THE future OF friendship

MOSAICA PRESS

THE future OF
friendship

Rebbetzin Feige Twerski

Published by Mosaica Press, Inc.
www.mosaicapress.com
info@mosaicapress.com

In loving memory of

רפאל בן ר׳ משה
צירל בת ר׳ מרדכי
Stern

Devoted to family and Jewish community
with great acts of *tzedakah* and *chessed*

In loving memory of

ריזל בת יעקב
יחזקאל בן אברהם
Salovesh

Deeply devoted to family and community

Their children
LISA AND ALAN STERN

I dedicate this book to my wife
Lotta Bea
because her life was enriched in so many ways
by the deep and lasting friendship she shared
with Rebbetzin Feige.

With warmest wishes for success,
STUART BRAFMAN

Table of Contents

PART III: Vision

PART IV: Mindfulness

PART V: Unity

PART VI: Gratitude

PART VII: Words and Action

Preface

I t is undeniable that these are unique times and that the recent pandemic has caused both lasting challenges and memorable opportunities. While these times bring a lot of uncertainty and sadness, the blessing of friendship, even in the midst of this unprecedented upheaval, remains a constant.

Unquestionably, we draw on the gift of friendship in our times of joy. A famous Irish poet once commented that "anyone can sympathize with the suffering of a friend, but it requires a very fine nature to sympathize with a friend's success."

It is also true that almost anyone can *sympathize* with the suffering of a friend, but not everyone is capable of *bringing solace* to the suffering of a friend; it is precisely in our most vulnerable moments that we need support, encouragement, and a shoulder upon which to lean.

One of my favorite and oft-quoted insights is that of the great Mirer Rosh Yeshivah, Rabbi Chaim Shmuelevitz, in an essay entitled, "*Mai'igra Rama l'Bira Amikta* [From a Vaulted Roof to a Very Deep Pit]." Rabbi Shmuelevitz addresses the painful chapter of Shaul HaMelech, King Saul, the first king of Israel, who lost his throne to King David after he failed to carry out G-d's instructions in the war with Israel's arch enemy, Amalek. When King Saul's mentor, Shmuel HaNavi, the prophet Samuel, came to tell Saul that his lapse in leadership was going to cost him the monarchy, Saul, who was the quintessentially humble person, pleaded with the prophet to *honor* him by appearing with him in the presence of the nation. Rabbi Shmuelevitz points out, most poignantly, that every human being encounters moments of misfortune and imperfection, situations where they need a friend, someone to hold onto, so that they won't slip into the abyss. King Saul recognized this danger and called on Shmuel HaNavi to be his support in an emotionally fragile time.

In less dramatic times, we depend on our friends for their honest feedback, wise counsel, sense of humor and just being there for us.

In a comment which echoes our heritage from the patriarch Abraham, someone once said, "Three things in human life are important: The first is to be kind, the second is to be kind, and the third is to be kind." In this vein, I wish to acknowledge those who, in their great kindness and devotion, helped make this book possible.

My wonderful friends, Yoni Schlussel and Ruthie Bryskier, who graciously typed my pieces without ever making me feel that I was imposing. Rechy Frankfurter, the editor of Ami Living, in which my weekly column upon which much of this book is based appears, for being a cherished friend.

Rabbi Yaacov Haber, Rabbi Doron Kornbluth, and their fabulously capable staff at Mosaica Press, for their professionalism, caring, and accessibility. And to my dedicated husband, who has painstakingly edited my words, not an inconsequential kindness for a person whose time is so demanding. In the scheme of all things, it may not seem like much, but as someone aptly observed, "Sometimes the smallest things take up the most room in your heart."

Finally, nothing happens without *siyata d'Shmaya*, the Heavenly assistance of the Ribbono Shel Olam, to Whom I am most grateful.

This book is dedicated to trying to make sense of, or better yet, achieve some sense of purpose in the lives of those who could easily be—and sometimes are—me and you. I hope it will resonate with you, my dear readers, and if it provides even a modicum of *chizuk*, I will be most gratified.

PART I

PERMANENCE

Chapter 1

How to Live Forever

D ebby appeared at my doorstep with red, swollen eyes. Choked with emotion, tears streaming down her face, she sobbed uncontrollably, unable to utter a sound.

When she finally regained her composure, she told me about her many recent losses. First, and by far the most serious, was the recent passing of her dear friend Lori. Before she'd even had time to wrap her mind around the catastrophic diagnosis, Lori was gone. Next, her family doctor and primary physician for decades retired. To add insult to injury, when she went to collect a prescription at the corner drugstore, where the old pharmacist knew all her family members by name, he told her that a large pharmaceutical chain had bought him out, and he was closing shop. The final insult came that very morning, when she looked out the window to find the County Forestry department cutting down all the trees on the block, victims of a scourge called Dutch elm disease.

The familiar landscape of Debby's life was rapidly shrinking and disappearing. She felt a growing emptiness and anxiety and was desperate to find something enduring to hold on to.

But what she was really lamenting was the impermanence of our existence. We all seek a stable and secure anchor in our lives. In pursuit of immortality, many invest in physical things—real estate, stocks, cars, artifacts, precious gems—in the hope of a semblance of permanence. Others try to still the shifting sands beneath their feet by creating relationships that give the illusion of something lasting. Finally, there are those who find no relief for their tortured souls other than self-destructive escape routes.

One of the Chassidic luminaries described a world of *tohu*, a world parallel to our own but utterly devoid of meaning and purpose. He characterized its inhabitants as people who try to convince themselves that everything in it will last forever. With that belief in place, they feel no need to set goals or strive for anything transcendent. The illusion of permanence blinds them to the need for a purpose-driven life.

Only the realization that time is limited motivates us to invest value into our moments.

I tried to tell Debby that while grieving over a lost past is appropriate, she needed to slowly transition into what she could do now to capture her time for eternity, to transform the temporal into the permanent. Lori had lived a life that brought cheer and goodness to others, I told Debby. She had given beyond herself and had left an indelible mark on everyone who crossed her path. Lori lives on, not only in the hearts and minds of friends like Debby, but in her acts of *chessed* that ascended with her to a place over which death has no dominion.

Ten months after the renowned Rabbi Moshe Halberstam, a leading member of the *Badatz*, passed away, he appeared to his son in a dream. The son inquired as to what was going on in the heavenly spheres. Reb Moshe responded that he wasn't permitted to divulge that much, but one thing he could say was that when one does a *chessed* for another Yid, it makes a great *roshem* (impression) in Heaven.

Gemilus chassadim (acts of kindness) are clearly of paramount importance in our reach for immortality. Debby was correct in her conclusion that nothing physical can be relied upon forever. The one exception is us; when we help others and dedicate ourselves to Hashem's will, our acts live on forever.

Chapter 2

Permanence

I t is common knowledge that life allows no one freedom from stress and challenge. In my many years of trying to help friends and family through seasons of hardship and suffering, it has become clear to me that everyone shares an underlying need for a constant and steadfast anchor they can turn to when the terrain of life changes and the familiar roads one has traveled are obscured.

In recognition of this phenomenon, secular author and social commentator Alvin Toffler wrote a book entitled *Future Shock*, predicting more than forty years ago many of the social casualties we would suffer because of rapid changes in our culture. Toffler noted that we live in a society where the familiar landscape and values by which we live today will no longer be relevant tomorrow. When Toffler's daughter returned empty-handed from a shopping trip to New York City because the store she had always shopped in was gone, Toffler observed that New York was becoming "a city without a history." He correctly identified the "future shock" phenomenon as one that augured "the death of permanence," one that heralded "a transient culture, where everything ranging from goods to human relationships would be temporary." These "rapid changes" have an almost vertigo effect on those of us who are trying to maintain our equilibrium in a kaleidoscopic environment.

5

Interestingly, the *sefarim ha'kedoshim* describe the times preceding the coming of Mashiach as so confusing, we will be hanging on by our fingernails.

I often think that if my father, who is gone for almost thirty years, would come back and see what has become of the world he knew, he would be gripped by horror and disbelief. So much of what was sacred and inviolable to him has been trampled by our culture with impunity. "Facebook friends" come and go—if they were ever really friends to begin with. Families are shattered. "Morality by consensus" is the god of our times. If the multitudes decide, so it shall be. There is no longer a higher authority that is respected. There is no objective transcendent standard that governs the lives of our society—anything goes. Criteria for dealing with both beginning- and end-of-life issues have reverted to the barbaric; to public policies that can only be described as signaling the end of a civilized world.

Almost thirty years ago, Mark, a secular, highly intelligent, and successful professional, walked into our Torah community with his family in tow and never left. Mark explained that the life he thought he'd signed up for—one where a friend was a friend, marriage was sacred, integrity was nonnegotiable, and family was a priority—was under siege. It had given way to the disintegration of the marriages of his contemporaries and the abandonment of traditional values that had made life secure and predictable. Mark was so shaken that he came seeking a sanctuary—a safe haven, anchor, and refuge from the "future shock" world of impermanence.

Over time, many others joined Mark in their quest for a life they could trust, and I can testify that many years later, they have reaped the dividends. Virtually all of these families now have children and grandchildren who are *shomrei Torah u'mitzvos* and are a *nachas* to behold! Unquestionably, the transition from the secular world, where the individual is the sole arbiter of what is right or wrong, acceptable or not acceptable, to a disciplined life circumscribed by Torah law was not easy. It required *mesiras nefesh*, sacrifices of the highest order. At the end of the day, however, their efforts have been vindicated. They feel a great sense of gratification that they and their children have become a faithful link in the golden chain of our eternal people.

My husband is fond of relating an anecdote about Pierre Renoir, one of the great French impressionistic painters, who later in life suffered from a very painful case of rheumatoid arthritis. On one occasion, he was visited by one of his famous students, Henri Matisse, who watched as Renoir put his brush to canvas, each time grimacing in pain. Noticing his agony, Matisse questioned why Renoir insisted on working at such great cost to his well-being. Renoir responded, "The pain will pass, but the beauty will remain." I am certain that many of our inspired *baalei teshuvah* would agree that many of the changes they made in their lives came at great personal sacrifice, but they would quickly add that the "pain passed and the beauty remained." The contemporary Torah world is well aware of the raging fires surrounding it, forces viciously attacking everything holy. Despite the virulence of the onslaught, we hold fast to a way of life that was, is, and will always be one that is immune to the "future shock" uprising that plagues the rest of society.

Mark summed up his escape to Torah by quoting David HaMelech's assertion in *Tehillim* (61:3–6): "From the end of the earth I call unto You, when my heart grows faint. Lead me to a rock that is too high for me to climb alone. For You have been a refuge for me, a tower of strength in the face of the enemy. May I dwell in Your tent forever, may I take refuge in the shelter of Your wings, Selah." I can't think of a more permanent, reliable, and durable place in which to hide in our mercurial, volatile world than Hashem's tent.

Chapter 3

What We Keep

Over the years, I have had the privilege of watching the different ways in which people plow through life's challenges. By and large, I have found that people manage their responsibilities with good judgment and reason, and most importantly, with well-balanced prioritization. For the more gifted, however, the issue of balance is especially difficult. The greater the talent, the more proficient the ability, the more likely one will be driven to explore all of their capabilities simultaneously. For the gifted, "success" is a highly seductive and harsh mistress, and I have watched many succumb to its blandishments. Whether it is money, power, glory, or popularity, for those blessed with talent, there is an ever-present danger of being sucked into a vortex of drivenness and ruinous imbalance.

The challenge of prioritization seems to be most problematic for our contemporary young people, who are juggling their complex lives and responding to the demands of spouse, children, extended family, career, and religious and communal obligations. I have often been distressed watching people trapped by the idea that they can do it all. Alas, when priorities are not assigned, the result is that individuals spread themselves too thin, and sooner or later, they pay a price for this overextension. Unfortunately, it is only when a crisis or catastrophe occurs,

Rachmana litzlan, that one is jolted into considering what really matters in life and is forced to introduce prioritization into their lives.

In a book entitled *What We Keep*, author Bill Shapiro addresses the question of what we would reach for if, G-d forbid, a calamity or natural disaster would occur and we would have to flee in a great hurry. The 2018 fires in California, where people lost their homes, along with everything they owned, was a case in point. Counterintuitive as it may be, he notes, people did not reach for their expensive belongings. Instead, they grabbed items that had sentimental value. "The heart is not an accountant," Shapiro states. When push comes to shove, people's most prized possessions are those that connect them to their past and that are of nostalgic value—the handwritten recipes of a beloved grandmother, an unremarkable bottle opener, a gift of a deceased grandfather. The things people grabbed as they fled were not the costliest, but the ones that gave them a sense of grounding and of connection. It was reported that fire fighters who responded to the 9/11 tragedy gingerly and lovingly removed photos from the ashes, knowing the comfort they would bring the bereaved families. "It's all just stuff," may be a true statement, but not all stuff is equal. There is indeed some stuff that is extremely consequential.

I recall hearing a touching story about the great Chassidic luminary, the Mezritcher Maggid, successor to the holy Baal Shem Tov and mentor to Europe's most distinguished Chassidic rebbes. The Maggid hailed from a prestigious family of rabbinic scholars and leaders, who traced their ancestry back to the kings of Israel. On one occasion, when the Maggid was still a youngster, the family home went up in flames, barely allowing the members of the family to escape the conflagration. As the young lad watched the fire, he noticed that his mother was crying. Surprised that a woman of his mother's exalted caliber would cry when it was mere "things" that were being destroyed, the Maggid confronted her, saying, "Mother, why would you cry over physical things?" "You are right, my son," she replied. "We are very fortunate that nobody was hurt. There was, however, a most valuable and irreplaceable item that was incinerated in the fire. It was our *yichus brif*, the parchment listing all of our illustrious forbears, dating back to *malchus Yisrael*."

The youngster looked up at his distressed mother and said comfortingly, "Well, Mama, I guess in that case, the *yichus*, our pedigree, will have to begin with me." The Maggid's insightful response underscores the importance of having durable priorities, values that remain with us when things of lesser significance no longer remain.

The point, as Shapiro suggests, is that we ask ourselves the question: If we had to leave and had only two minutes to decide, what, aside from family, would we grab? This exercise might also help us gain perspective. We are surrounded by an incredible amount of "stuff," which we spend so much precious time accumulating. At the end of the day, how much of it is just "stuff" and not worth the effort that is required to amass it. We can use this question as a litmus test to reorder our priorities and invest in pursuits of which no natural disaster can rob us, i.e., meaningful relationships with our spouse, children, parents, siblings, and friends. And, of course, the value of giving to others. Clearly, that which we give away—resources, time, and caring—no force on earth can take from us. They are ours forever.

The distractions of our time are perhaps more powerful than at any other time in history. In the midst of massive confusion and chaos, we are called upon to make cogent, balanced, and decisive choices that are consistent with the values of our faith. This is no simple matter, and awareness of its gravity is the beginning of dealing with the challenges it represents. May Hashem bless us with clarity and courage to bring order to our priorities, to spend more time connecting to our friends and loved ones, and to invest our lives with true substance and meaning.

Chapter 4
The Meaningful

The transient nature of life is undeniable. It surfaces in bold strokes in every aspect of life, from the very significant to that which should not, but does, affect us greatly.

My husband and I take an occasional break in the Palm Springs area of California. Dear friends accommodate us with the use of their beautiful home, where we can rest and recharge our batteries. The surroundings are quiet and peaceful. The natural beauty of the local environs gives amplified meaning to David HaMelech's exclamation: "*Mah rabu maasecha Hashem*—How glorious are the works of Your Hands, Hashem" (*Tehillim* 104:24).

Our children usually take turns coming to spend time with us there, trying to make sure that we navigate our older years without mishap. In addition, it gives them a chance to have quality time with us, while simultaneously observing the mitzvah of *kibbud av v'eim*.

In an effort to be mindful of our physical health, my daughters and I have taken walks that, besides the cardiovascular benefits, enable us to visit some of the local shops. Over the years, I have made friends with some of the saleswomen. Even though my purchases have been meager, these women, many of whom are Jewish, relished the opportunity to spend time sharing their stories. A painful aspect of developing these relationships is that when I have gone looking for these women in sub-sequent years, slowly but surely, they have disappeared from the scene, having retired or passed on. I swallow hard when given this information and perforce move on. Admittedly, they were peripheral to my life, but they were friends nonetheless, and their absence confirms to me how fleeting life can be.

The most important part of our lives is, of course, the people in them. Still, aside from people who come and go in our lives, there is the familiar landscape, the institutions and objects, that enjoy but a brief moment in the sun and then recede into obscurity.

Consider the expression, a "Kodak moment," an idiom coined when the film in cameras captured precious moments. There was a time when film had to be removed from one's luggage at airport security points. Not only is that era gone, but the new generation is not even aware that such a thing as film existed. Much the same fate has been shared by rotary phones, phone booths, and telephone landlines, which are also becoming increasingly extinct. Along with the phenomenon of what was and no longer is are the companies and people who have invested their resources and energies in the promulgation of these products, who have similarly become obsolete.

Hence, in addition to the wisdom of living in the moment, there is the issue, or better yet the challenge, of how and what to invest in, as we look to the future. Huge companies and department stores that dominated the commercial scene in the not-so-distant past are folding or dramatically downsizing. Economists are trying to figure out why in-dustries coalesce around some cities and not others. In our fast-moving economy, new businesses seem to sprout up on the horizon abruptly, having become "incubators" for new ideas. Yet, when the idea becomes sufficiently mature, it surrenders to those who churn out new success stories. It is the classic *galgal ha'chozer*, the wheel of fortune, at work. One moment a company or a person can find themselves on the top, and a figurative moment later, the wheel turns, and the heretofore enjoyed success is no more than a passing memory.

Thus is the nature of the physical and material world. *"Anu ameilim v'heim ameilim—*We toil and they toil," we state when celebrating the conclusion of a volume of the Talmud. The text continues, "We receive reward and they [the nations of the world] do not receive reward." The explanation of this puzzling statement is that in the secular world one only receives reward for their toil if they "succeed." If a salesperson or company is profitable, they endure and are rewarded. If not, they fail and there is no compensation. All has been in vain, an exercise in futility. In the world of Torah and mitzvos, however, every modicum of effort is rewarded. It is the toil, the *ameilus*, that counts and is precious to the Ribbono Shel Olam. "Success" is not measured by the outcome or the ends, but by the means, the process, the journey. Every moment invested in the pursuit of a spiritual goal is already a success. None of our investments therein will become obsolete, because they belong to the realm of *nitzchiyus*, of the eternal, where expiration, decay, and death have no dominion.

In a most poignant tribute to his recently deceased young wife, Rabbi Doniel Chaim Alter, a brilliant scion of the Ger dynasty, offered the following parable. He spoke of a king who, in honor of his birthday, issued a decree that for a short period of time he would entertain requests by a select number of his subjects who might be granted an audience to see him. A poverty-stricken villager managed to be among the few chosen to present themselves to the king. He related to his sovereign that he had a large family and no resources and asked if perhaps the king might appoint him to a village office from which he might support his family. The king was impressed by the sincerity and the modest request of the supplicant and instructed the poor fellow to return home. Crestfallen and heartbroken, the petitioner returned to his home. Upon his return, he was greeted by a great surprise: The king had sent a royal carriage to carry him to become the governor of an entire province, a gift beyond his wildest dreams.

Reb Doniel Chaim concluded by saying that, indeed, he and others had pleaded for long and healthy years in this world for his beloved wife. The request as stated was not granted. Instead, in the eternal world of everlasting good, the Almighty granted her a far greater office, a far more exalted experience of "life" and blessing.

Reb Doniel Chaim's remarks highlight the stark difference between the choices that confront us moment to moment. While all of us importune Hashem for the good physical things we would like to have in our life, and hope our Heavenly Father will grant our wishes, nevertheless, we must not lose sight of the fact that our primary investments should be in the relationships we have, and in the eternal verities that will grant wealth and joy beyond anything that we can even imagine.

Chapter 5

Relationships

A seventy-five-year-long Harvard study was released some time ago. The topic of the study was the issue of "meaning" in life, i.e., what brought people fulfillment in life, what gave them a sense of purpose and personal value. In research that social scientists consider one of the most exhaustive explorations of this type ever undertaken, the researchers interviewed people of every social, economic, and occupational status. Over the duration of almost three-quarters of a century, they followed their subjects with interviews and questionnaires to document their progress.

In the end, the Harvard researchers found that the most central and essential factor in attaining meaning and joy in one's life was neither money nor fame nor power. It was *relationships*. Many of the respondents confessed that their initial thinking was that the pursuit of money, fame, and fortune would deliver the sense of purpose they sought. They discovered, many not soon enough, the void and ultimate futility of these pursuits. At the end of the day, it left them with nothing to assuage the existential need to matter. Moreover, the study noted unequivocally that on the whole, people in strong relationships lived longer and enjoyed better health. Indeed, at a very basic level, what worked in their favor was that they had a reason to live.

Loneliness is one of the most serious afflictions of our time. People can be surrounded by many others, belong to clubs and fraternities, professional guilds, large families, or be married, and still experience profound loneliness. The key determinant in achieving a real relationship is the quality of the connection, the extent of the investment in the other, and the mutuality of the give and take. A somewhat surprising finding was that even couples that spent years bickering and experiencing the ups and downs of marriage, still fared reasonably well. Anger, disappointment, and contrariness, barring toxic abuse, did not negate the benefits of a relationship.

For B'nei Yisrael, gifted with the *Torah ha'kedoshah*, the idea that relationships are central to happiness comes as no surprise, as we have been aware of their critical role for thousands of years. At the very outset of the creation of man, the Torah states: "*Lo tov heyos ha'adam levado*—It is not good for man to be alone" (*Bereishis* 2:18). Our Sages expound on this verse, commenting that a person alone dwells "without blessing, without good, and without joy." Man, Hashem states, was not *meant* to be alone. While marriage is a primary relationship, relationships are not exclusive to marriage. In addition to it, significant relationships are built with friends and family. There is a whole other layer to relationships: the supreme relationship to cultivate is the one between ourselves and the Ribbono Shel Olam.

I had occasion recently to observe two elderly couples. The husbands were dealing with serious health issues, and the prognosis in both cases, according to their physicians, was very grim. Both, however, defied the doctors' predictions and miraculously rallied. Although the doctors are mystified, their circle of friends are not. The curative factor, we know, is that they each have a supportive and caring spouse at their side. Geriatric psychologists have observed time and again that residents in the homes for the aged who reach out to others and invest in creating and cultivating friendships are more likely to maintain their health and well-being and to live longer than their less social counterparts.

A close friend of ours, Harlan Loeb of Chicago, Illinois, commented during a recent visit on what is being recognized as one of the greatest impediments to contemporary relationships: *smartphones*. Increasingly, they distract us from being fully present with others. Talking on the phone frequently, looking at emails, checking missed calls, texting, and keeping up with YouTube while in the presence of another person can be a virtual death blow to a relationship. Harlan shared that a recent study showed that even casually holding a phone in one's hand, without even using it, delivers the message that one is not totally engaged in or connected to the encounter with the other.

Clearly, relationships are where our focus should be. The good news is that investing in others can happen in small increments. Hashem assures us: *"Pischu li pesach k'pischo shel machat v'ani eftach lachem pesach k'pischa shel ulam."* All we have to do, we are told, is "make an opening the size of the eye of a needle," and Hashem will make for us "an opening the size of a doorway to a large hall." We merely have to begin the process with a small act of caring.

Heavenly assistance, we are assured, will be forthcoming. A kind word, a compliment, an act of generosity, and acknowledging another person will go a long way.

Chapter 6
Legacies

There is a saying: "If you don't heal from what hurts you, you will bleed on those who didn't cut you."

There is a profound truth to this statement. Over my many years in counseling, I have seen the casualties of those who did not address the source of their pain, and as a result ended up visiting their misery upon innocent others, usually their friends and family.

- Devorah came from a dysfunctional home and was subjected to the unfortunate role of being a pawn in her parents' divorce. The trauma of her parents' impervious disregard of her well-being affected her ability in her own marriage to fully believe that her husband's devotion was real. Devorah interpreted every behavior that did not totally meet her expectations as "abuse." To her, they constituted overtones of her primary relationship with her parents, who had grievously betrayed her.

- Amy's mother was an icon in her community, the head of every "do-good" organization in town. Instead of Amy feeling proud of her mother, she felt neglected. She felt that she did not rate as a priority in her mother's life. As a result, Amy was left with a deep gash in her sense of self-worth, a gash that manifested itself, subsequently, with multiple complications in her marriage.

- Ahuva was the only child of a Holocaust survivor. Her father was unreasonably strict with her, making no allowances in her adolescent years for normal teenage escapades. Hard as she tried, Ahuva could never do anything right or ever earn his approval. This culminated in sadness and depression that escorted her into her adult life.

- Sandy's mother was left all alone to raise her after the war years. Sandy, an only child, was the object of all her mother's hopes and dreams. It was a huge burden and Sandy was subjected to constant criticism. Sandy felt that she could never quite measure up. It was only after her mother's death that she found a note from her mother, in which she apologized with an explanation that at the root of her often-abusive treatment was love and a desire for Sandy to realize her full potential. All the good intentions notwithstanding, Sandy is still trying to recover, while her family bears the brunt of her emotional bruises.

Terrence Real, a noted psychotherapist, provides an important takeaway message for all of us. He states: "Family pathology rolls from generation to generation, taking down everything in its path like a fire in the woods, until one person in one generation has the courage to turn and face the flames. That person brings peace to the ancestors and spares the children that follow." Real concludes that we either "pass it on or pass it forward." This means that in confronting and facing our painful past, we are then in a position to stop the cycle of negativity and abuse. We can choose to raise our children and model a totally different paradigm for them, and to be an example to our friends and community. Most importantly, children learn what they live. We have a choice of raising our children in an environment where we can help them face toward the light, in contrast to our own painful experience.

Sarah is a young woman I have never met, but calls periodically for guidance and support. Her mother, she relates, lives geographically a considerable distance from her but still manages to heap abuse on her from afar. Sarah is always concerned about the parameters of her Torah obligation to her mother. What has always impressed me is that Sarah assures me that her mother's behavior has been extremely instructive, as she has learned what *never* to do in her relationship with her own children. Sarah is determined to break the destructive pattern that has plagued her family for generations.

The Torah states that "Hashem remembers the infraction of parents for either three or four generations," but only, our Sages explain, if the children perpetuate the parent's behavior. While this Divine principle is understood to apply to infractions of Torah and mitzvos, our collective experience shows that it applies to the way in which the emotional abuse of parents gets passed on, as well.

We can excuse our pathologic and destructive behaviors by arguing that it's not our fault, that this is the legacy we were handed, and consequently, the one with which we are most conversant. Or we can "face the flames," avail ourselves of the necessary resources, counseling, and guidance, and create a new life-affirming legacy, which will benefit not only those who succeed us, but ourselves, as well.

As the saying goes, "Nobody promised us a rose garden." The path for each of us to create a better example for those around us and a healthier legacy for our children is challenging and difficult. Then again, what is the alternative?

Chapter 7

Patience

If history proves anything, it is that mankind has learned little from history. In a widely quoted aphorism, the poet George Santayana warned: "Those who do not remember the past are condemned to repeat it." From everything we read and hear these days, our world is not remembering, and is indeed repeating millennia of terrible blunders. There is nothing new about the observation that "haste makes waste," and the indisputable fact of life that impulsive behavior guarantees a multiplicity of mistakes. Over the last half century, with the unprecedented progression of technology, our culture has become less and less tolerant of caution and circumspection, and more and more insistent on speed and rapidity. Many social scientists have lamented our society's obsession with instant gratification and quick fixes. Maybe it's my imagination, but it seems to me that ever larger numbers of children are being diagnosed with ADD and ADHD, conditions that are reflected in many adults who have lost the requisite patience and stick-to-itiveness to patiently and diligently stay with a program over an extended period of time.

We want what we want, now, quickly.

My brother-in-law, Rabbi Dr. Abraham J. Twerski, addressed this very issue years ago. He commented that this phenomenon is captured by the ad that shows a hassled woman preparing dinner for her husband's boss. She is nervous and already stressed to the max when she discovers that her sink is plugged up. The gist of the ad is, "Don't suffer, take Advil to relieve your stress." My brother-in-law observed that this was so typical—a quick fix! "How ridiculous," he declared. The ad should have urged: "Ma'am, you have a backed-up sink. For goodness sake, call a plumber! Address the root of your problem!"

In a similar vein, an addiction specialist summarized his patients resorting to drugs to deal with their unhappiness by commenting, "It's like you're standing on a nail and you take morphine so you won't feel the pain. Clearly, morphine is not the solution. For goodness sake, get your foot off the nail. Look for the root cause!"

I was guilty of pursuing a quick fix recently. I had carpal tunnel syndrome for years. This last Yom Tov season, with its labor-intensive demands, was particularly challenging. The pain, particularly at night, was excruciating and prevented me from sleeping. As it happened, I read about a group of doctors who had developed a minimally invasive treatment that promised a ten-minute procedure and practically no recovery time. Although I researched it, I was blindsided to the red flags I should have seen. I went for it.

It was a disastrous choice, and this many weeks later I still haven't recovered. The assurance that this was a shortcut with no downtime was too much to resist. Thankfully, this is not a life-threatening issue. Nevertheless, it does speak to the reluctance to address the core issue and pay the price required to engage a legitimate course of action.

My friend David has a more serious issue. He allows himself time and again to be drawn into counter-indicated relationships that have exacted a huge toll on his life. He already has several children from different wives. Though advised repeatedly to avoid women who are addicted to drugs, alcohol, or other self-destructive behaviors, he has eschewed caution and listened to no one. Currently, he is once again attracted to a loser, who like himself has not sought help for the core issue in her life. His pursuit of yet another relationship, toxic as it may turn out to be, is a desperate attempt to put a Band-Aid on the underlying condition that requires serious and long-term intervention.

The Torah value, as expressed by our Sages, is "*l'fum tzara agra*," commensurate with one's pain is the reward. The reward in sorting out any given situation in our lives is dependent on the effort we are willing to expend. We need to be wary of those who make hollow promises of a quick fix, with offers of immediate gratification.

Alas, the above attitude extends to marriages as well. The divorce rate in the *chareidi* world has skyrocketed in the last number of years. Unquestionably, many of these divorces could not have been averted. However, many marriages *could* have been salvaged if the couple would have been willing to hang in there and put forth the necessary effort. It seems like it is harder and harder for us to put in the time and patience necessary to build solid relationships, whether with friends or loved ones.

Study after study shows that the key to long-term happiness and growth is relationships. A few good friends, and a person is set for life. A solid marriage, and a person is set for life. So why don't we work harder to achieve these connections?

My father-in-law, *a"h*, once recounted his experience with a couple who had sought his counsel and services. He had strongly advised them not to divorce. Despite his direction, the wife insisted on pursuing the divorce. Some years later, my father-in-law met the woman who had initiated the divorce and had since remarried. In response to my father-in-law's inquiry about how she was doing, she replied that she would confide in the Rabbi something she would never admit to anyone else. She said that if in her first marriage she had been willing to put forth the amount of work she had invested in her current marriage, it would undeniably have been superior to her current one.

Leonard Loeb, *a"h*, who was one of Wisconsin's leading family law attorneys and a devoted friend, never agreed to preside over a divorce proceeding if the couple had not first sought counseling. He would often divert these people to our doorstep. Leonard's assessment of what he encountered day to day was that the "dirty" four-letter-word in our society was *work*. He elaborated by saying that when he introduced to the troubled couple the concept of working on their relationship, it was like speaking a foreign language to the listeners.

The common denominator in all the above cases is that patience, stick-to-itiveness, and the willingness to work hard to achieve a goal is in very short supply in our driven, instant-result world.

Awareness of this troubling phenomenon should give us pause before deciding on any meaningful course of action. We would do well to reflect on what we are about to do, to ask ourselves what attracts us to the option we are considering. Are we addressing the core issue productively, or are we getting sucked into something easier and quicker that can have devastating results?

PART II

THE HEART

Chapter 8

An Understanding Heart

D
r. Irvin David Yalom is an American existential psychiatrist whose practice is largely devoted to helping terminally ill patients through this anguishing period in their lives. Over time, he discovered that he has been far more successful with these patients than some of his younger colleagues.

When he explored the reason why this was so, he found that it was due to his being older, and as such, more aware of his own mortality. His patients felt that their confrontation with mortality and the therapist's advanced age was a common denominator. Mortality acted as a bridge between them.

True understanding, it appears, is much more than an *intellectual* grasp of information and the ability to process it cerebrally. The younger therapists were well-equipped with that quality of thinking, but nonetheless were unable to "connect." The older psychiatrist, on the other hand, had an understanding heart and a deeper, more intuitive appreciation of the situation, which proved helpful in the interactions with his patients.

Our Sages confirm this fact of life. There is none wiser than the one who is similarly challenged.

The following metaphor once offered by my husband captures this unique understanding: Dennis, a doctoral candidate in anthropology, was researching a small, relatively unknown tribe deep in the African continent as the topic for his doctoral dissertation. As a serious academic, Dennis did extensive research on every aspect of their culture. He became extremely knowledgeable about the tribe's life-cycle rituals, their demography, their agriculture and economy, their language, eating habits, and legal system.

Harry, another doctoral candidate, took an interest in this very same tribe. After considerable scholarly inquiry, he felt dissatisfied with the academic information he had collected. He picked himself up and traveled to that corner of the globe, spending a lengthy period of time with the natives of the tribe, experiencing life with them. Predictably, he became attached to them.

Some years later, the two students learned that a devastating earthquake had struck the region and destroyed the entire tribe and its village. Dennis was moderately distressed by the event. Harry, who had lived among them and had established meaningful relationships with them, was inconsolable.

Clearly, the difference between Dennis's and Harry's reactions was that Dennis was invested in intellect alone, whereas Harry was invested with mind and heart, and was therefore stirred to the core of his emotions.

The centrality of bringing an understanding heart to one's industry was evident in the construction of the *Mishkan*, the place where Hashem and man would meet. The Torah tells us that *"chachmei lev,"* the wise of heart, were sought out to be its builders. One might have assumed that "the wise of mind" would be most desired for this critical task, but despite the importance of the gifts of reason, the Torah identified *emotional intelligence* as the critical component in this most exalted of undertakings.

The relevance of all of this for the contemporary Jew is urgent. Our society is drowning in a veritable ocean of verbiage. Never before have we been surrounded by so many words, so much information, assaulting us from every possible direction, and yet so many people today feel that nobody is listening. More and more people complain that they feel socially isolated and alone.

To counteract this phenomenon, we must recognize the imperative of being fully present and engaged in our daily interactions with others. We must prioritize relationships. It speaks to the necessity for extending a listening heart in our interaction with those around us. In a culture of distractions, this is no small feat. Our spouses, children, and friends suffer all too often from oblique attention, when they desperately require meaningful interaction with their loved ones.

Dr. Menninger, a noted psychiatrist, was called late one night by a young woman who was seriously contemplating suicide. For the better part of an hour, he presented her with the many reasons for which she should go on living. At the conclusion of their conversation, he urged her to come to his office first thing in the morning.

To his delight, she actually appeared at the designated time, whereupon Dr. Menninger was able to more effectively probe into the roots of her despair. He asked if she would identify for him which of the arguments during the previous evening's telephone call had convinced her to go on living.

After a moment's reflection, she responded that it was not any particular point that touched her, but the willingness of a man of his stature taking the time to talk to her. It made her feel worthy enough to move forward in her tortured life. For her bruised psyche, it provided the desperately needed vote of confidence in her value as a worthwhile human being.

All of us have the wherewithal, if we so choose, to warm the hearts of others, not unlike Dr. Yalom, who climbed into the darkness with his patients and made them feel understood and supported. If we so wish, we too can devote undistracted, caring time to others, like Dr.

Menninger, who revived the spirit of his suicidal patient to give her the gift of life.

All of us can cultivate a listening heart and the wisdom of the heart by climbing out of ourselves and our personal distractions, noticing others and life around us. What is needed is that we slow down to the "speed of life," as it was meant to be experienced and lived, and go through life *together* with our friends and family and the One Above.

Chapter 9

A Product of the Heart

Over the years, we have watched the youngsters in our community grow up to become fine young men and women. They are a great source of *nachas* to us. The young men have, for the most part, after their graduation in Milwaukee, gone on to various yeshivos where learning Torah is the main focus. This is certainly as it should be, and how fortunate we are that our young men aspire to that lofty goal.

At times, however, I have heard my husband lament the fact that these *bachurim* could be benefiting even more from their learning experience, if they would but amplify their study with a *relationship consciousness*.

My husband directed me to the *sefer Nefesh HaChaim* by Rav Chaim of Volozhin, where he states that *limud haTorah*, the accumulation of Torah information, is a worthy goal under all circumstances. He notes, however, that one should approach Torah study as *chochmas haBorei*, the wisdom of the Creator, and not merely as another intellectual pursuit. Implicit in this statement is the principle that both mind *and* heart need to be applied in order to connect to the Creator, of whose wisdom we are the beneficiaries. Connecting and forging a relationship with the Source is the game changer from merely gleaning information to gaining Torah knowledge that teaches, inspires, and guides.

Many *sefarim* note that the information of the Torah is referred to as the *guf*, the body of Torah, whereas the *neshamah*, the soul of Torah—the pivot of the **relationship** with Hashem—is accessed by looking for Him in the encrypted messages of these sacred words. Both mind and heart are required for the journey into the depth of Torah. The Talmud (*Shabbos* 105a) expresses this by saying: "*Ana nafshi kesivas yahavis*—You will find My Soul [says Hashem] in the letters of the Torah." This represents an unmistakable invitation to look beyond the words and seek the relationship that can thus be forged.

Unquestionably, an even greater challenge facing all of us, young and old alike, is that of davening—our daily prayers, referred to as *avodah she'ba'lev*, the **work** of the heart. In this case, *avodah* implies hard work. We are all familiar with the legion distractions that regularly disrupt and claim our attention during *tefillah*. Nonetheless, we are called upon to persevere because davening constitutes the auspicious privilege of an audience with our Heavenly Father, who loves us and is eager to connect with us.

It should be noted that prayer takes many forms and shapes. Formal *tefillah* is not the only available medium. Opportunities abound every moment to address the Ribbono Shel Olam with either requests or expressions of gratitude: "Please, Hashem, send me good news from the hospital"; "Please, Hashem, let Moishele do well on his test"; "Thank you, Hashem, for making me go downstairs to look for my charger last night, in the process of which I found the meatballs I had neglected to put in the fridge that would have spoiled by morning."

These are all legitimate prayers.

Our son Rabbi Benzion once shared an insight into why Aharon HaKohen, Israel's high priest, was instructed to stand on a stool when performing his task of lighting the Menorah in the Beis Hamikdash. It seemed unnecessary, he observed, since the Menorah was no taller than an average person, and thus easily accessible.

The answer he gave was that Aharon HaKohen, still haunted by his "complicity" in the sin of the golden calf, felt unworthy of the great privilege of performing this exalted mitzvah, of lighting the holy Menorah of the *Mishkan*. He was therefore charged with standing on the stool, metaphorically lifting himself up and not allowing the lesser part of himself, his inner critic, to deter him from his *avodah* and destroy his fervor.

Similarly, in order for us to become invested in davening, we need to lift ourselves above any negative self-talk—and negative attitudes from our friends and acquaintances—which is certain to derail us.

An anecdote is told of the Baal Shem Tov. He arrived at a village one afternoon, during one of his travels. He sought out a shul in which to daven the *Minchah* prayer, yet when he found one and opened the door, he drew back, explaining to his chassidim that it was so crowded, there was no room for them to enter. One chassid, puzzled by the fact that at midday a shul would be so crowded, opened the door and found the place to be totally empty. When he asked the Rebbe for an explanation, the Rebbe answered that heartfelt emotions provide our prayers with wings to soar heavenward. If, however, prayers are said mindlessly, they remain in the space in which they were recited, hence, the crowded shul. After hearing this story, I was much relieved to learn that the Baal HaTanya mitigated its harshness by commenting that even if most of our prayers lack the requisite input of heart and mind, the minute we invest in one *tefillah* appropriately, it carries all the previous ones aloft.

A story that lingers in my mind from my childhood underscores this concept even more. It tells how a great *tzaddik* was informed during his davening that there was a young lad in a neighboring village whose prayers were more favored in Heaven than his. Intrigued by the fact that a young lad had managed such an achievement, the *tzaddik* traveled to the boy's village to learn his secret. When the *tzaddik* arrived there, he was told that the lad in question was a shepherd, who could be found with his sheep in the outlying pastures around the village. The *tzaddik* made his way to the outskirts of town, where he might observe the young lad's prayers from a discreet distance. From his place of hiding, the *tzaddik* heard the lad exclaim, "Merciful Father in heaven, You have been extremely loving and generous to me. I am grateful for all Your bountiful gifts, my health, my clothes, my food, my livelihood, the sheep and the meadows, and your beautiful world. As You know, You took my parents from me when I was very little. Being an orphan, I had no one to teach me Your Torah or how to daven. But before my father died, he taught me the letters of the *aleph-beis*. So I am going to recite all the letters of the *aleph-beis* again and again, and You will take them and make up the words that find favor in Your eyes, and bring blessing on Your nation, Israel." With that, the lad began to shout the *aleph-beis* with all his heart and might, and as he continued to repeat the letters with great joy and fervor, the *tzaddik* understood why Heaven found the boy's *tefillos* far better than his own.

Torah learning and davening that are devoid of heart and soul, while not inconsequential, are not the ideal. At the end of the day, the presence of Hashem resides deep within us, far beyond that which meets the eye, and can best be accessed by focus of our minds and the longing of our hearts.

Chapter 10
A Broken Heart

D uring my more than fifty years as a communal rebbetzin, I have had occasion to observe people's reaction to the traumatic events that are an inescapable part of the human condition. Most devastating among them is the experience of loss: the death of a loved one, catastrophic illness, loss of *parnassah*, dissolution of a marriage, children off the *derech*, and alienation from children, friends, and family.

Psychologists draw a distinction between being heartbroken, and one's heart being "broken open":

- Being "broken open," one philosopher notes, "opens us up and lets out all the greatness we hold within."
- "Heartbrokenness" that is indulged for too long a period of time locks one in a dark dungeon, impenetrable to light.

Our son Rabbi Benzion, in a recent *derashah* to our community, referenced the example of the *Nesiim*, the princes of the tribes of B'nei Yisrael. He noted the fact that the *Mishkan*, the Sanctuary, was built with the free-will contributions of B'nei Yisrael. The *Nesiim* elected to wait and see what would still be needed after all the donations had been collected. They would then step in to fill in the rest from their private coffers. To their great chagrin, they found that the nation had contributed everything that was required, and there was nothing left for them to add. The *Nesiim* were heartbroken over the missed opportunity. When it came time to ritually inaugurate the *Mishkan*, the *Nesiim* were eager to make up for their mistake. They stepped forward with rich and elaborate offerings for the initiation of the *Mizbei'ach*, all of which are recorded in painstaking detail in the text of the Torah. The instructive comment of our Sages is that the *Nesiim* did not wallow in their state of heartbrokenness. Instead, when one door closed for them, they sought another avenue through which to serve Hashem.

Rabbi Benzion quoted the following parable from the Imrei Emes of the Gerrer dynasty:

> *A young man sought to curry the favor of his father-in-law. In an effort to do so, he went to an exclusive gift shop to find an impressive item to give him. Everything he looked at, however, was beyond his price range. The proprietor, noticing the customer's frustration, asked him if he might be of assistance. The young man spilled out his story to the sympathetic owner.*
>
> *"I have an idea," replied the proprietor. "I have a very expensive crystal vase that broke earlier today and is beyond repair. I saved the shards in a box to be disposed of, and you can have them at very little cost. I will put them in a gift box and you can take the box to your father-in-law. Just as you approach the door, simulate a fall, drop the box, and pretend that the impact was what broke the vase. Your father-in-law will see the value of the crystal shards and will certainly appreciate the sentiment of your present."*
>
> *Excited by the brilliant plan, the young man followed suit. When his father-in-law opened the box to see the present his devoted son-in-law had brought him, he found the broken shards. However, the store owner had wrapped each fragment in a separate piece of paper—and the ruse was up.*

When asked what the message was, the Imrei Emes responded with the following succinct words: "A broken heart." Indeed, a broken heart, which is a product of acknowledging our shortcomings, and our subsequent remorse is very precious to the Ribbono Shel Olam. The caveat, however, is that the gift of the broken heart should not be wrapped up and indulged endlessly. Rather, it should propel us to seek other alternatives for growth. We should move from a "broken heart" to a "heart broken open."

This small change in phrase makes all the difference.

- Consider the example of Lizzy, who succumbed to an unfortunate temptation as a young woman. Though she subsequently was blessed with children and grandchildren, she carried her "broken heart" with her into her every relationship. It robbed her of the joy that she might have legitimately enjoyed. It tainted her every interaction and erected an impenetrable stone wall around her heart. Sadly, it shut out those who could and should have been the nearest and dearest in her life. Her heart remained broken, not broken open.

- In contrast to Lizzy, there was Carrie, who also capitulated to an indiscretion and, though equally heartbroken, embarked on a life dedicated to meeting the needs of those less fortunate than herself. Carrie visited the sick, checked in on the lonely, drove the homebound to stores and appointments, shopped for moms with newborns, and helped the elderly and the handicapped with their laundry She did not allow the shards of her life to define her.

Understandably, all of us experience heartbreaking moments in our lives, times when we are disappointed in ourselves and our behaviors. The Ribbono Shel Olam is not interested in offerings of neatly packed shards, remnants of our broken hearts. Indeed, He is looking for us to experience the brokenness of pain and shattered dreams, but only as an impetus to motivate us to reclaim our integrity by finding a new path, a path blazed by the *Nesiim* and all the luminaries throughout the ages whose examples inspire us. The message to ourselves and our friends is that the path forward is indeed *forward*.

Chapter 11

The Stone Age

T he mind-body connection has been receiving increasingly greater credibility in the medical community. Dr. John Sarno, a noted orthopedist, wrote several books and treated thousands of patients for a condition he called TMS, contending that ubiquitous back pain and other ailments of our time are psychosomatic at their root—meaning that the pain is induced by repressed and unresolved emotional issues. According to Dr. Sarno, the very awareness that subconscious forces are the provocateurs in and of itself, relieves countless people from debilitating pain. Many refuse to accept this premise and seek alternative measures to deal with their suffering, only to discover that the psyche has generated new sites of discomfort.

Be that as it may, it is noteworthy that our generation is referred to in our sacred literature as the *ikvesa d'Meshicha*, literally, the "heel of history," the era preceding the time of Mashiach. The commentators point out that the heel, in addition to being the lowest extremity of the human body, is also characterized by dead skin. They expound that in the "time of the heel," emotions, feelings, and responses will be dulled and colorless.

Evidence that this "blunting" is manifest in our times is the fact that our moral sensibilities are progressively assaulted by changes in culture without evoking any expression of protest or indignation. It seems that we do not feel as deeply as people once felt. Clearly, the age of *eikev* is upon us.

In our *eikev* generation, we get caught up in the wonders of science and technology, of computers and social media, that eliminate much personal human contact and exacerbate the dearth of emotion. Everyone feels vulnerable, hesitant to expose oneself as a human being. The analytical mind reigns supreme, leaving intuitive emotional intelligence undervalued and the spiritual realm abandoned.

All types of friendships and relationships have suffered, because at the end of the day, acknowledged or not, a human being is not a machine. Though we live in an age of emotional repression, when push comes to shove all of us need nurturing. We all need to know that we matter, that someone cares about us.

Parents often call me to seek counsel about a proposed *shidduch*. The jargon usually consists of his being the best boy and top learner in Yeshivas XYZ. I break into a sweat, because there is no mention of *mentschlichkeit*, of *middos tovos* or kindness. I typically advise that what they describe sounds like a great candidate for a *chavrusa*, but a husband cannot merely be the human counterpart to a computer. My husband has often noted that one would not stand up for a computer in which the entirety of Torah was encoded. Without a heart, without emotions, without *middos tovos*, a computer is nothing more than a collection of matter, with no inherent holiness.

Unquestionably, the emotional component is indispensable in any relationship. Cheryl is a perfect example. She spends most Yamim Tovim with her son Michael. Her other son, Eli, is seldom on her radar. I gently inquired why she favors one over the other. Unabashedly, Cheryl responded that Michael's wife and children make her feel wanted, needed, and appreciated. They call her to keep her in the loop, apprise her of the latest news, from toilet-training stories about the younger ones to *shidduch* possibilities for the older ones. The grandchildren respond to the packages she sends with effusive calls of gratitude. They repeatedly request that she knit them the beautiful blankets that are her trademark.

Recently, I accompanied Cheryl on a shopping trip. She purchased large quantities of cereals and informed me that she was going to send them to Michael's family. Innocently, I pointed out that the postage was going to cost far more than the cereals themselves. Wouldn't it make more sense to send them the money and let them buy the cereals themselves? After a few lame attempts to defend the logic of the shipment, she conceded that while my objection was true, the children loved getting packages from her. They have come to associate all good things as coming from their beloved Bubby.

Skip the reasoning, the analysis, the rational mind—it is the heart and emotions that trump everything. The Torah refers to the truly wise as *chachmei lev*, wise of heart, for no matter how far afield the *ikvesa d'Meshicha* may take us, that is still where ultimate wisdom resides.

Chapter 12
Matters
of the Heart

There are things in our life that touch us so deeply, they cannot be captured by words. They are matters of the heart.

I had one such experience on a ten-day visit to Camp Arugas Habosem, the Tzeilemer camp in South Fallsburg, New York, with my sister and brother-in-law, the Tzeilemer Rav and Rebbetzin. Because I live far from New York and am busy around the clock with the needs of my own community, I rarely have an opportunity to spend quality time with my sister.

We tend to forget how gratifying it can be to spend time in the company of someone whose soul vibrates to the same rhythm as our own. To the extent that human utterances can be pressed into service, the visit was something I can only describe as a balm for my heart. The bond I share with my sister transcends articulation; it is a relationship that reminds me of the adage, "The heart has reasons that no reason can know."

The exaggerated veneration of the sciences and worship of the intellect that has consumed our culture for the past century is slowly giving way to an appreciation of the intuitive mind. Alternative healing disciplines, for example, are gaining respectability in the mainstream community, to the extent that many modalities once scorned by mainstream medicine are now covered by health insurance.

It is becoming more and more apparent, even to hard-nosed empiricists, that the human being is not a one-dimensional entity. Phenomena that can be tested and proven in a lab are only one aspect of the forces that constitute a person.

Abby came to us for advice about the young man she was seeing. She was very distraught because on paper he was everything she wanted, but her visceral instinct told her otherwise. "Which is more reliable," she asked, "facts on the ground or the more intangible feelings that make me uneasy?" Knowing Abby to be a solid young woman with no phobia of commitment, we advised her to stay in touch with her intuition and proceed with great caution.

Another case that comes to mind is that of Barbara, a warmhearted, highly educated woman who had been diagnosed at a very young age with a life-threatening disease. Barbara researched every available resource for the most effective treatment, traveling at great cost to faraway places that boasted the best physicians in the field. When it came to making decisions about her treatment, she told us, her litmus test was the *feeling* she had about a particular doctor and the staff members who worked with him or her. If the doctor was considered the most qualified but her gut told her otherwise, she was out of there in a hurry.

Barbara had originally been given six months to live, and she attributed the fact that she had lived for another eighteen years to her belief that life cannot be reduced to science alone.

Rabbi Joseph Ber Soloveitchik, an imposing figure on the Jewish scene for much of the last century, was a person of great intellect and a prominent Talmudic scholar. Despite his dominant analytic faculties, he was also a very intuitive individual. In a poignant address many years ago, he stated that on the last Simchas Torah of his beloved wife's life, he knew that she wouldn't be with him much longer because as he was taking the *Sefer Torah* out of the *aron kodesh*, it dropped from his hands to the floor of the *aron*. Then and there, he said, his heart informed him that she wasn't going to survive her illness.

"*Libi omer li*—My heart tells me," is a statement often made by *Rashi* and other elucidators of Torah when their comments draw on insights that go beyond a collection of demonstrable facts.

It is widely recognized that women have this gift of intuition in far greater measure than men. In discussing the creation of Chavah, when the Torah states, "*Va'yiven Hashem Elokim es ha'tzela*—And Hashem fashioned of the side" (*Bereishis* 2:22), our Sages interpret this to mean that women are endowed with a *binah yeseirah*; the word *binah* derives from the same root word as the word "*va'yiven*" and refers to an intuitive grasp of situations.

The Talmud in *Berachos* draws attention to the incident of the Shunamite woman, who discerned that her guest, Elisha the prophet, was a holy man—a fact that had escaped her husband. The Talmud concludes that women, by virtue of their extra intuitive sense, are more attuned to people's character.

I have shared with many audiences the fact that my father often used to request my mother's presence in counseling sessions. He used to advise us half-jokingly, "Listen carefully to what your mother is saying now, because in three weeks it will be my opinion." Coming from a man of exceptional brilliance, his statement was a tribute to a woman's unparalleled insight.

I have heard many rabbinic leaders and teachers lament the fact that *avodah she'balev*, serving Hashem with our hearts, especially in regard to davening, has become one of the most difficult achievements for our "cerebrally acculturated" generation. Reawakening the heart and restoring its connection to the brain is one of the most critical challenges facing our generation.

In conclusion, matters of the heart are not to be dismissed cavalierly. A human being is neither a computer nor a repository of antiseptic facts. The quality of emotional intelligence is much more valuable. It is this capacity that, more than anything else, will build our relationships, which are so important to our lives.

Chapter 13

The Loan of Life

"Some refuse the loan of life to avoid the debt of death," a psychiatrist noted after a lifetime of working with clients. He was referring to the phenomenon of people refusing to engage fully in life and in creating and maintaining relationships because of the inevitability of losing them.

- Sandra had been married happily for twenty years when her husband died after a protracted illness. She was devastated, but she pulled herself together heroically in an effort to take care of her household and five children. Nevertheless, there was an undercurrent of sadness that accompanied her every move. After a number of years, friends began to suggest marriage possibilities for her. Although she appreciated everyone's concern, she rebuffed these attempts, unwilling to consider remarrying. In our conversations, it became clear that having loved and lost, she would not entertain the idea of taking this risk again. She could not see investing her heart and soul in another relationship that might be taken from her, because if that happened, it would only reopen and intensify the original wound, which had never really healed. Sandra refused the "loan of life to avoid the debt of death."

- I observed a similar dynamic with my friend Libby. Libby had married a man considerably older than herself, and they had enjoyed a wonderful life together. However, when he went into partial retirement at seventy and began to spend more time at home, she started to feel unaccountably irritated with him. She felt herself withdrawing, to the point of entertaining fantasies of separation. What emerged in our discussions was that Libby had never gotten over the pain of her mother's death, which had torn her apart when she was a very young child. She did not want to have to face the agony of another grievous loss. It was clear to me that she was trying to protect herself from the pain of losing her husband by reducing her attachment to him. I suggested that neither her anger nor her withdrawal were effective ways of coping with loss, although they are not uncommon. Many of us probably know someone who has become numb to life and avoids living with gusto for fear of losing too much.

- Another intriguing example is Leah, who left an abusive marriage of many years and was fortunate shortly thereafter to meet a wonderful man. Having come to see herself as deserving of suffering, Leah proceeded to sabotage the relationship, putting all sorts of impediments in the way so that it would not move forward. In our talks it was obvious that she was waiting for the other shoe to drop. After all the misery she had endured, she could not permit herself to trust anyone for fear of being disappointed again.

- Dana was happily married for over forty years when her husband suffered a crippling stroke. As time passed, his health deteriorated, and she was forced to place her beloved husband in a nursing home. Facing a serious void, Dana adopted a different coping strategy. She went into a spin of feverish activity with siblings and friends, trying to drown out the thought of life without her devoted companion. Subconsciously, she was using distraction to avoid dealing with the inevitable, but the dynamic was the same; she distanced herself from the "loan of life" so that she would not have to pay the "debt of death."

• Finally, there is Shaindy, a generous person who has room in her heart for everyone's needs. Shaindy always dreads the end of the Yamim Tovim, especially Simchas Torah, during which the joy and celebration in our community are nothing short of magical. Young and old, children, grandchildren, in-towners, and out-of-towners all rejoice with the Torah in an explosion of *simchah*. The atmosphere is electric. Virtually everybody turns out for the davening and *hakafos*, but Shaindy has consistently chosen to absent herself, explaining that she can't tolerate the letdown in the days after the festivities are over.

All of these women, in one way or another, are like a person who is given the gift of an ocean cruise but stays in the cabin all day, refusing to meet fellow travelers or to enjoy activities, in order to avoid the disappointment of the end of the cruise.

Of course, these women's concerns are completely understandable. Life can be hard. At the same time, however, the Torah offers a refreshingly different perspective. We are instructed: *"U'vacharta ba'chayim*—And you shall choose life." The Torah recognizes that there will be times in our lives when the emotional stakes are so high that we will want to retreat from life so as not to risk more pain and anguish. Nevertheless, the Torah insists that we choose life and engage in it fully.

Implicit in the exhortation to choose life is the premise that every moment we are granted is a privilege. Hashem presents us with these moments, trusting that we will invest them with purpose and meaning. It is His wish that we fill our precious few years on this earth with all the love, connections, relationships, meaning, and energy we can muster.

PART III

VISION

Chapter 14
A Different Kind of Simchah

G iven the proclivity of today's media to focus predominantly on the world's tragedies, and the speed at which technology brings distressing news to our immediate attention, I like to focus on the positive.

This isn't easy. We are too often drawn to talking, with both friends and family, about the negative. Unfortunately, this imbalance is also reflected in our rabbinic service, where people tend to bring us their problems, and sometimes forget to inform us of their good fortune. It seems that we expect and feel entitled to the good, and feel unfairly attacked by the bad—leaving us with no need to talk about the good. In truth, both the good and the bad represent opportunities and challenges to our integrity, and both demand that we respond to them with a Torah perspective.

While we generally tend to define *simchahs* as events and happenings in the lives of our family and friends, I would urge us to consider a category of *simchahs* that are the product of personal achievement. There is wisdom in the idea that everyone should have some activity or goal in their life that is an expression of their creative juices. For young women, it is enough that they give themselves unselfishly to their growing families. Their *simchahs* come from the daily victories over the myriad challenges of keeping their homes secure and afloat. These heroic wives and mothers deserve a daily mazel tov for their successes. For more mature women and empty nesters, celebrating their personal *simchahs* of self-expression is a challenge no less formidable than that facing younger people. The difficulty notwithstanding, I believe it is extremely important for *bnos Yisrael* in this stage of life to find ways to experience the singular joys—the *simchahs*, if you will—of developing and expressing their individual callings. This pursuit may be reflected in a variety of ways, such as volunteering to be of service to the elderly, tutoring children who need extra help, participating in *bikur cholim* activities, joining a book club, developing creative talents like writing, drawing, or singing, or best yet, whenever convenient, babysitting their grandchildren.

I hope that it is evident to all that the objective in my writing is to connect with people on an experiential level. I believe that when one scratches beneath the surface, we are more alike than we are different. We are all trying to make sense out of life, our relationships, our connection to Hashem, dealing with our friends, spouses, children, and friends. In addition, there are the ongoing struggles of making a living and maintaining our health and well-being. Having been "around the block" a few times (a euphemism for being a senior citizen), and having been in the field of counseling, I have been given a window into people's lives and their travails. As I encounter these, I try to give others strength and guidance through them, as it is rare that someone else's problems do not have some correspondence, however remote, with our own challenges and dilemmas.

I've often quoted my husband's response to one of the *mispallelim* in our shul who accused my husband of directing his *derashah* remarks specifically at him. My husband answered that, in fact, he was speaking out loud to *himself* and allowing others to eavesdrop. I share that sentiment. Both in my oral presentations and in my writing, I convey that which resonates with me, with the conviction that insights that work for me will most likely be appreciated by others, as well.

As a rule, I take the pain of others more deeply and personally than is good for me. I want more than anything to assuage their pain and make their load a bit lighter. At the same time, I am forever impressed with the courage and resilience of those I have encountered who have so much on their plate and meet their tribulations with incredible faith and joy. Those ongoing victories are also occasions of simchah, and deserve an ongoing mazel tov. I have often assured my friends who say I have offered them much that, in truth, they have offered much more. Isn't this what friendship is all about?

Chapter 15

How We Look at Things

"Things aren't as they are, they are as we are" is an observation that gets confirmed over and over again in my experience. The implicit meaning is that all of us view events from our own biased perspective. Invariably, personal agendas twist our field of vision and judgment, and unfortunately, all too often, this is to our great detriment.

Representative of the above are the following cases:

- Tzippy, a young, vivacious grandmother and long-time friend, called recently to share with me her anger and frustration. Tzippy recounted how her son was marrying off his first child, Elisheva. Elisheva was Tzippy's first grandchild and the apple of her eye. Being a very popular girl, when Elisheva reached marriageable age, she was bombarded with all kinds of promising matches. Among the many *shidduch* options that presented themselves, Tzippy's son chose a young man who, in Tzippy's estimation, was not of the caliber she had hoped for. Tzippy felt that her son had been blindsided by the wealth of the *chassan*'s family, and that her son had settled for money over quality. Tzippy was heartbroken by the choice and lamented how easily a less-than-ideal situation could be rationalized. From her perspective, her son's personal agenda compromised his field of vision.

- Tamara's problem was internal family strife. It began when one of her brothers took offense by what he perceived to be a serious affront to his *kavod* by another sibling. It didn't take very long before the other siblings took sides and intense rancor developed. As a result, family *simchahs* and gatherings no longer had the wonderful flavor of togetherness that had previously prevailed. To the extent that each side was hopelessly invested in their position, the chasm became unbridgeable, and the parents, who had heretofore been so proud of their children's close bond, suffered enormously. The children did not see that their "righteous indignation" was driven by ego and self-interest, and that their vision was obscured by their biased perspectives.

It is refreshing to note, in stark contrast, the innocent and unadulterated perspective of a child. Children have the ability to cut to the chase, and to see things for what they really are.

> *Benzion, my seven-year-old grandson, has always been a deep thinker. After the recent wedding of his uncle, his mother asked him about his impression of the wedding. Benzion reported that he was particularly touched by the chassan's crying under the chuppah. "What were you thinking, Benzion?" his mother asked. "I was thinking," Benzion responded, "that the chassan was doing teshuvah (repentance) for his aveiros (sins), so I too decided to repent for my aveiros." My grandson, so little yet so wise, then concluded, "I saw a tear drop from the chassan's eye, and I moved quickly to let that precious tear fall on my hand. I then wiped my face with it because, unquestionably, it was a heilige (holy) tear."*

The weltanschauung and vision of a child is so refreshingly pristine and uncluttered that we wish it would last forever. Life, for the most part, has not yet exacted its toll on their perception.

In our morning davening, in the *Shemoneh Esreh*, our first petition to the Ribbono Shel Olam is for *seichel*, wisdom. "*Atah chonen l'adam daas*—You grace us, Hashem, with wisdom and understanding." We then qualify this request, however, by asking, "*Chaneinu **mei'itcha** chochmah binah v'daas*—Let it be **from You**, Your version of truth," i.e., we want the real deal and not our limited view of that which is before us.

May Hashem bless us with Heavenly directed insights through which we may discharge our responsibilities. May He grant us the wisdom that will serve as a reliable compass by which we will be able to successfully navigate our journey in this challenging sea we call life.

Chapter 16
The Danger of Judging Others

Every year, the mourning of the period of *sefirah* helps us get ready for receiving the Torah on Shavuos. It was during *sefirah* that twenty-four thousand students of the great Rabbi Akiva died in a plague. We are told that the reason was that "*lo nahagu kavod zeh la'zeh*," they didn't treat each other with the appropriate honor and deference. Given their exalted spiritual stature, they should have known better. One of the takeaway messages for all of us—and this is relevant the entire year!—is that we cannot expect to really receive the Torah without taking a good, hard look at ourselves.

A case in point occurred recently when we were in Israel. When Dafna's husband, Ari, a dear soul, began to experience deteriorating health, she found herself his sole caregiver both day and night, since the couple had no children, family, or adequate resources. Eventually, the demands of the situation became untenable. The circumstances confronting Dafna led her to not only support, but encourage, her husband's plan to stop eating and drinking, and thus bring an end to his misery.

On our last visit with Ari, we pleaded with him to continue living. He listened to us and seemed to agree that life, despite all of its challenges, was still worth living. He perked up, energized by our assurance that not only G-d, but we too, cared about him, loved him, and wanted him in our world. Dafna, however, was visibly distraught and distressed by our visit. In fact, she sent us a message that under no circumstances were we to contact her husband again. Clearly, her plan to allow him to die was in danger of being thwarted. Predictably, a number of weeks later we received word that Ari had passed away.

Aside from mourning a person who had long ago been an integral part of our lives, I found myself resenting Dafna, who in my opinion had defaulted on her role as a sustainer of life. Upon examining my feelings, however, I realized how unfair my assessment was. Dafna had been a devoted wife; a good and decent person, who was dedicated to Ari's care around the clock. After what must have seemed an interminable amount of time, her energies were depleted and there was nothing left of her. Perhaps she was a product, as we all are, of our human limitations.

Besides the fact that judging another person is inexcusable, grievous, and wrong, it also opens us up to the dangerous possibility of inviting similar situations into our lives, G-d forbid. In a sense, Heaven's response to our judging others is that if we are so quick to judge someone else, "let's see what *you* would do under similar circumstances." That possibility alone should give us great pause.

In Biblical times, someone who spoke ill of another person was afflicted with a supranatural skin eruption called *tzaraas*, and was relegated to banishment outside the encampment of the community of Israel. In a sense, the diminished standing in society the gossiper's slander caused his victim was now being visited upon the perpetrator. Because he sought to create a barrier between this hapless individual and the rest of society, justice dictated that he would now get a taste of his own medicine by being subjected to a similar state of isolation.

The many complicated variables of another's life are never ours to know. The ultimate wrong is to set ourselves up as judge and jury of another person. Moreover, the pain and hurt inflicted on others by jumping to conclusions can have lasting effects.

Consider Dina, a longtime friend. She was a youngster when she came to America with her family following the horrific war years. As the eldest of eight children, she'd had to assume much of the burden of raising them. Her mother was sickly and overwhelmed. At only ten years of age, Dina had to awaken, dress, and feed her siblings every morning before sending them off to school. Only then could she put herself together and get going. As a result, she would invariably be a few minutes late. Her teacher, respected in the system as a very competent educator, excoriated her pupil mercilessly for her tardiness. Not once did she make an attempt to find out why Dina, an otherwise exemplary student, would present with a behavior that was clearly out of character. Dina, a proud and stoic child, never pleaded her case, but always felt that her teacher had poured salt on her wounds. Not only did she have excessive responsibilities for a child her age, but she also had to bear the brunt of the wrath of a misguided and clueless adult. Fifty years later, she was still feeling the impact of someone who had judged her without knowing all the facts. When this teacher was subsequently honored for her extraordinary achievements, Dina chuckled and prayed to G-d that she would never be given a similar test, for fear that she might fail to understand that there is much in other peoples' lives we don't know.

May Hashem help us learn from our past mistakes. May He help us understand that only in being unified with our fellow Jews, "*k'ish echad b'lev echad*—like one man with one heart," without judging them, will we merit to receive His greatest gift and treasure, our holy Torah.

Chapter 17

The View from the Window

fter resisting cataract surgery for several years, I finally surrendered to my ophthalmologist's insistence that I have the cataract removed. This past week I had my vision corrected with an artificial lens. *Baruch Hashem*, it went well, and my eye is healing nicely. On my follow-up appointment, my ophthalmologist asked me if the world was looking brighter now.

This was not a philosophical question; the doctor was certainly not inquiring whether my clearer vision had affected my perspective on life. But even if he had not intended it that way, perhaps this deeper context was something I should consider. Hashem is constantly sending us messages in many different ways, and perhaps this was a message for me.

What came to mind was the well-known anecdote of a woman who looked out her kitchen window to see a neighbor's wash hanging on the line to dry in the summer sun. The woman commented with disgust that the clothing was still quite dirty, and she launched into a diatribe about poor household management. Her children went out to play, and a few minutes later they came back in to tell their mother that the neighbor's wash was perfectly clean—but that her own windows were streaked and dirty!

The message is obvious. It is much more effective to correct our own faulty vision than to indulge a jaundiced outlook on other people and situations. Psychologists have noted that what seems to matter in the end is not so much what happens to us but how we *perceive* what happens to us, how we see the truth of our lives. That perception becomes the world in which we live and act. In other words, we live in our minds and hearts.

This truth is well illustrated by the story of Mimi, a young acquaintance of mine who lost her mother. Afterward, there was a family reunion; Mimi and her three sisters sat around the old kitchen table reminiscing about their shared past. They were feeling especially close and tenderhearted:

- Chaya, the oldest sibling, looked at the refrigerator and said, "I can still see Mom standing there, pouring me a glass of milk. Do you remember that sweet thing she used to do when she got us a glass of milk? She'd take a sip first to make sure it wasn't spoiled."
- Shayna, the second daughter, the one with the analytical mind, raised her eyebrows. "Mom did *not* sip our milk to test for freshness. She did it because she always overfilled the cup. Her spatial judgment was a little off."
- Debra, the sardonic third sister, looked at her siblings as though they had no clue. "You're both wrong," she said. "Mom was stealing our milk."

"So what have we learned about our mom from this story?" Mimi wondered out loud. "Was she a devoted caregiver, a person who was somewhat uncoordinated, or someone who would steal milk out of the mouths of her children? We'll never know. But in the end, it doesn't really matter."

We all have separate realities that are determined by how we see and interpret the facts of our lives. Mimi's siblings experienced the same situation with totally disparate interpretations.

In the same way, a trauma that makes one person a monster turns another into a hero.

I learned recently about Mrs. Gottlieb, a warm, generous woman in Brooklyn whose two daughters, one married and the other a young teenager, were killed in a tragic car accident—a devastating experience that no mother should ever go through. No one would have blamed Mrs. Gottlieb if this calamity had turned her into a bitter person. But Mrs. Gottlieb is not an ordinary person. She chose instead to honor the memory of her beloved daughters by creating a life-affirming vehicle for *chessed*—an affordable gown *gemach* to enhance the *simchah* of young brides. Although Divine Providence did not allow her the privilege of celebrating the wedding of her second daughter, she was determined to do whatever she could to bring joy to others marrying off their children.

Mrs. Gottlieb chose a perspective that was forward-directed. As long as the Ribbono Shel Olam blesses her with life, she is resolute in her desire to shower goodness and blessing on those around her. For all her quiet modesty, she is a true hero.

In many cases, an incident may be considered a gift by one person and a curse by another. What I may hear as a compliment, you might hear as an insult. The bottom line is that if we try to see things with generous eyes—searching for the truth, but then bestowing upon the truth the brightest and most charitable interpretation—we can come to perceive a more beautiful world.

Cataract surgery can lift the cloudy film from one's eyes. More important for our general well-being, however, is to remove the blinders that prevent us from seeing and appreciating the many blessings that surround us. How do we see our friends? How do we see our lives? It is certainly Hashem's intention that we live joyously and gratefully, which can only happen when we see the world with benevolence.

When we recite the *berachah Pokei'ach Ivrim* each morning, thanking G-d for our ability to see, we might also ask Him to open our eyes to the bounty in every aspect of our lives. May Hashem remove our spiritual cataracts so that we may find Him and His goodness wherever we look.

Chapter 18

One Step at a Time

What can we really do to help our friends in their struggles? After all, *they* need to go through their struggles, not us.

Of course, there is plenty to do. We can daven for them. We can hold their hands and let them know we care for them. And we can share an important life attitude with them, over and over. If it rubs off on them even a little bit, we will have lived up to the word "friend."

What am I referring to? One of the most important Torah objectives for the Jewish People is to keep growing. Hashem's first recorded exhortation to Avraham Avinu, the patriarch of our nation, was "*Lech lecha.*" *Lech* means "go," i.e., to travel, keep moving; while *lecha* means "to you," i.e., for *your own* sake, to actualize *your* potential. Thus began the mission of, not the *wandering* Jew, but the *journeying* Jew. With *lech lecha* ringing in the ears of every one of Avraham Avinu's progeny, the demand to eschew remaining stagnant or settling into a place of complacency has become the marching order for every Jew. There is a caveat, however, that cautions that growth has to happen in measured steps if it is to be sustainable. Leaping ahead with an enthusiastic desire to do what we believe Hashem wants is commendable, but care must be taken to gradually and deliberately integrate that which we seek to acquire. Growth in small increments is the approach that is most likely to succeed.

My husband once explained that the reason the Torah orders that the *Mizbei'ach* in the Beis Hamikdash have a ramp, rather than steps, is to teach us this valuable lesson. On a ramp, the Kohanim were able to ascend by placing toe to heel. In contrast, steps would require them to separate their feet as they go up. The Torah's proscription against steps emphasizes that growth *requires* small, incremental moves that allow for organic and healthy integration.

Many years ago, we mentored Judy, a very bright secular young woman, who was drawn to embrace a Torah observant life. Despite our warnings, Judy jumped headlong and full force into every *chumrah* and *minhag*, which she eagerly devoured in her relentless religious studies. She approached every aspect of her new life with a burning intensity that, while some would have deemed it praiseworthy, was guaranteed to backfire and explode. When it finally did, we were not at all surprised at her subsequent religious estrangement. Like anything in life, going too quickly can often lead to going in reverse! Haven't we all seen this struggle in ourselves and our friends?

In our early days of counseling, when I began to apprentice with my husband, I learned a fascinating lesson. People would typically unload problems so daunting that my heart would sink. I could not imagine that their situation was salvageable. On one occasion, I told my husband that the only solution I could see was that this couple should be born again with a clean slate. Remarkably, though, I watched my husband as he suggested that they make a small change—a minuscule step—in the right direction. I groaned inwardly. To me it felt like putting a band-aid on a raging hemorrhage. To my great surprise, when they returned the following week, they were glowing. "Things are so much better, Rabbi," they announced. I was totally mystified. I came to learn that a great truth was at the core of this experience. The secret is that success breeds success; that a move in the right direction, however modest, proves to us that we can do it. And if we can make one change, we discover that we have the absolute wherewithal to do more.

Conversely, grabbing too much at once, however well-intentioned, sets one up for certain failure. This is not an uncommon pitfall with yeshiva *bachurim* and young spiritual aspirants who, when determined to reach for the skies, commit to learning many consecutive hours a day without a break. Predictably, extreme assiduousness cannot last and sadly leads to a loss of heart, wherein these young men consider themselves failures. Experience has proved, time and time again, that taking on too much all at once is a recipe for disaster.

Our daughter Ruchel shared a story she had read in one of the popular women's periodicals. The story was about a taxi driver in Israel by the name of Chabib, who, while transporting a passenger, was uncharacteristically quiet. The passenger, throwing discretion to the wind, inquisitively asked the driver if he was an observant Jew. The taxi driver obliged him with the following response: He and his wife were chain smokers. When anyone tried to suggest a more traditional life, such as keeping Shabbos, they knew it could never happen because they believed it was impossible for them to survive twenty-four hours without smoking cigarettes. On one occasion, Chabib continued, he was driving on a street where some Breslover chassidim were doing their thing. Dressed in white, their tzitzis flying as they jumped and twirled, they were dancing to lively music on a busy corner. When the taxi slowed to stop at a red light on the corner, one of the chassidim approached the taxi, knocked on the window, and extended a small *sefer*. Chabib declined, saying he had no money to pay for it. The Breslover chassid deposited the *sefer* on the passenger seat just as the light turned green, and the taxi drove off. At the next red light, the driver peered at the pamphlet and was startled by what jumped out at him. In bold letters, it stated that if one smokes just one cigarette less than they are accustomed to on Shabbos, it is most precious to the Ribbono Shel Olam.

Chabib went home and consulted with his wife about this astounding revelation, and they decided to use the one-cigarette-less approach for the coming Shabbos. On Friday, Chabib urged his wife to light Shabbos candles, and after a quick meal, he suggested that they both go to sleep early so that they wouldn't succumb to the compulsion to smoke.

On Shabbos day, after the meal, struggling hard not to cave in, they decided to take a long afternoon nap. When they got up, they figured that they could muster the strength to hold out till the end of the day, and resorted, instead, to eating pepitas on their porch. Henceforth, Chabib concluded, since they discovered that they were equal to the challenge, he and his wife became *shomer Shabbos*.

The secret to Chabib's success was learning that a small act, a small step, mattered in the eyes of Heaven. Upon examination, this "secret" is found in the pages of the Talmud (*Yoma* 80a): "*Tafasta merubah, lo tafasta*," which teaches that one should not try to grasp too much. Life confirms this admonition because, invariably, one who violates this principle achieves nothing. In sum, progress begins with a small step.

People are sometimes (often?) overwhelmed by the vastness of the tasks they face. We usually experience this when we unload our burdens to our friends, and they unload theirs to us.

When we hear a little voice in our head telling us that we have to do it all, we would do well to dismiss it. The urge to "do it all" is the voice of the *yetzer hara* trying to derail us from following an effective path to success. The quiet voice that counsels us to pursue one small, integrated step, is the voice of reason, the voice of *kedushah*. Following this path will certainly lead us all the way to the top of the *Mizbei'ach*, with the coming of Mashiach in the very near future.

Focusing on this life-attitude is one of the greatest gifts we can give our friends—and ourselves.

Chapter 19

Attitude

I am constantly struck by the separate realities in which people experience their existence.

Batya, a lovely, elegant, and intelligent elderly woman, recently stopped in to chat and solicit an opinion. Her issue was that although she was genuinely grateful for the blessings of children and grandchildren, she found herself almost dreading upcoming *simchahs*. She was expected to travel great distances from one child to the other, adjusting to new locations, new beds, lively environments, irregular eating schedules and late hours. She lamented the fact that as the years passed, her energy levels had diminished to the point that she was often depleted and worn out. Batya felt that she was stuck "between a rock and a hard place." On the one hand, she didn't want to disappoint her children or in any way detract from their joy. But at the same time, she didn't know what to do with her feelings of listlessness and exhaustion.

Ironically, I was visited a few minutes later by a contemporary of Batya's, who was her polar opposite. Between sobs, Annie, who had never married, bemoaned the family she'd never had and felt that her life was devoid of purpose. Her friends were always going off to family *simchahs*, and while she was frequently invited to others' affairs, it wasn't the same as if it had been her own children or grandchildren.

Two reasonable, normal people. Two completely diverse realities.

On a lighter note, I see this phenomenon playing out among my own children every summer. Some of them cannot wait to escape the city and go up to the country to enjoy the fresh air and let their children to roam free. Conversely, there are those who literally detest the mountain experience: the mud tracked into the bungalows, the cramped quarters, the lack of privacy, husbands and wives separated for much of the week, leaky roofs, and legions of insects. The only reason they go, they claim, is for the sake of the little ones, who thrive in the open space and fresh air.

Parenthetically, one of my daughters, now married, *baruch Hashem*, has never let me forget that I forced her to go to summer camp at an early age. To this day, so many years later, she insists that she is still suffering from post-traumatic stress disorder triggered by that experience. Some of my children would actually pack their bags every night, hoping they would find someone who might take them home. Yet some of their siblings relished going to camp and enjoyed every minute of the activities and the opportunity to make new friends.

Go figure. Apparently, there is no "one size fits all" when it comes to reality.

There is, however, an understanding that if grasped and integrated into one's consciousness can offer relief for Batya, Annie, and those of my children who felt victimized.

The concept is very simple. It is the indisputable fact that all of our feelings—dread on Batya's part, deprivation by Annie, "abuse" by my children and yes, even happy anticipation on their siblings' part—all originate in their thinking. It is our *thinking* about the circumstances in which we find ourselves that generates our feelings about them. We mistakenly imagine that our situation gives rise to the way we interact with life, but it's actually the way we choose to think about it that does. At various stages of our lives, we have no doubt felt differently about the very same set of circumstances. The only difference was how we thought about what was happening. In other words, we live in our minds.

The great benefit this understanding provides, I explained to both Batya and Annie, is that it puts *them* in the driver's seat. They don't have to feel trapped by circumstances that are clearly not always in their control. While in this particular moment, they feel down and out, perhaps their next thought will be a positive one that will liberate them.

Unquestionably, the separate realities in which people live must be respected. We are never in a position to judge others. But for us and those in our sphere of influence, availing ourselves of the understanding of how we function as human beings can be a game changer.

My father, *a"h*, used to say that this is the meaning of our assertion in the morning davening that Hashem is "*mechadesh b'chol yom tamid maaseh bereishis*," that He renews the act of creation on a daily basis. His explanation was that although the world out there appears to be the same as yesterday, Hashem gives us the ability to be *mechadesh*, to renew our world by virtue of our attitude and thinking. The outer trappings, the circumstances, will be the same, but our reality, the product of our thinking, will be vastly altered.

While we may not always be successful in tapping into this understanding, it is always available to us. The choice is ours.

Chapter 20

Farginners' Club

E veryone is familiar with the phenomenon where a small event or occurrence triggers a flood of memories. That happened to me recently when a dear friend, Claire Ciss of Toronto, Canada, called to touch base. In the course of our conversation, Claire shared that she had come across a photograph of one of my daughter's weddings, where my father, *a"h*, was dancing the *mitzvah tantz* with his granddaughter. It was a blurry picture, Claire said, perhaps, she speculated, because it was over thirty years old, and as such, it was not a prime candidate for a painting. Claire, however, as an extremely gifted artist, saw it as a challenge and felt there was an aura about this picture that she wanted to capture. When the painting arrived in the mail, I was transported back in time. Even though my father is gone now for several decades, his memory and legacy escorts all of us—his children, grandchildren, and great-grandchildren—every step along our journey in life.

My father, the Faltichener Rav, had a powerful impact on the many who were privileged to know him. My father used to feel great distress that we don't have enough card-carrying members of the "Farginners' Club." Claire's painting caught my father's ecstatic joy in the blessing of his granddaughter's *simchah*, but it was a joy that radiated from his face at the weddings and *simchahs* of friends and distant relatives as well, because my father was a real *farginner*.

Farginner is a Yiddish word, which, in its closest translation into English, describes someone who does not begrudge others their good fortune. My father noted that since we all have credit cards, such as Visa and MasterCard, which provide us with manifold financial benefits, we should also carry a Farginners' Card, which denotes our membership in an elite club espousing *farginner* values. This, he said, would entail celebrating and congratulating friends and acquaintances when they are blessed with good fortune, such as finding a good *shidduch* for their children, finding the means to build a new addition to their home, or when their children's special achievements give them great *nachas*. *Farginners* do this even when their hearts are heavy with a desire to have those very blessings in their own lives. Pull that Farginners' Club card out of your wallet, my father would say, and make a call wishing the fortunate individual well. My father insisted that if we would institute this practice, it would create a bond of *achdus*, of togetherness, that the Ribbono Shel Olam could not ignore. Hashem would not need to resort to other, less pleasant means, to remind us that we are one.

This message struck me as especially relevant because I was still reeling from an interview I had heard of a prominent psychologist, which discussed the growing phenomenon that experts refer to as "opportunity hoarding."

This unfortunate posture is one of sabotaging the opportunities others might have in advancing their well-being—whether getting into the best of schools, finding the best buys, or other similar opportunities—by keeping information "close to their vest." Opportunity hoarders thus prevent others from accessing good fortune in any and every field of endeavor in the mistaken notion that they must hoard it all for themselves. Moreover, they feel that if others succeed, they will somehow be diminished. The said psychologist noted that this describes a culture that is increasingly self-absorbed, self-indulgent, and uncaring about the welfare of others.

On a recent visit, our seven-year-old grandson, Avrumi, posed the following question at our Shabbos table. He had learned in cheder that Har

Sinai, the mountain on which the Torah was given, was the lowest and least imposing of all the mountains, and that all the towering mountain peaks vied for the honor of being the mountain upon which the Torah would be given. Avrumi, the little philosopher, juxtaposed this with the account of Yaakov Avinu when he fell asleep at Beis El. We are informed that in that episode, when Yaakov prepared to go to sleep, he placed many stones at the head of his "bed." The midrash says that the stones all sought to be the one upon which the great *tzaddik* would place his head, and in the end, they all merged into one big stone and the dilemma was resolved. Why, Avrumi asked, didn't the mountains do the same? Why didn't they all unite and become one? In a response, wise beyond his seven years, Avrumi decided that none of the stones were seeking to exclude the others; they were perfectly satisfied to be part of the whole. The mountains, however, sought to be the exclusive site of this special event, arrogantly rejecting all the others. Thus, none of them merited to be the choice of the Ribbono Shel Olam, Who loves humility.

Little Avrumi intuited correctly what the "opportunity hoarders" have yet to learn. When we come together as one, when we look out for the well-being of our friends, family, and even strangers, we all benefit. It's a win-win situation. Mankind needs to adopt an abundance mentality. There is no scarcity in the treasure house of the Ribbono Shel Olam. Indeed, the best way to begin the process of implementing the *achdus* necessary for the receiving of the Torah, "as one person with one heart," is to become a card-holding member of the Farginners' Club.

Although this reads easily, I know from experience that it does not come easily.

What if, realistically speaking, our hearts are not fully engaged? What should we do? To that, my father would respond, "Behavior is what matters." We must, as the saying goes, "Fake it until we make it."

I suspect that after 120 years, when we arrive at the gates of Heaven, what may be demanded of us as a means of identification—rather than a driver's license or credit card—will be a Farginners' Club Card. That would be a sure sign that throughout our lives, we believed in Hashem's providence and abundant goodness, and wanted the best for those around us.

Chapter 21
It All Depends on Me

O ur *sefarim ha'kedoshim* describe our relationship with the Ribbono Shel Olam as taking two distinct forms. The first is that of *avadim*, where we are subjects in G-d's kingdom, created to toil in His service. In this aspect of the relationship, we are called upon to abide by the dictates of His rule, just as citizens in a country must mind the dictates of their monarch, no questions asked. The second dimension of our relationship with Hashem is that of *banim*, where we are children in His Divine family, and He is *Avinu she'ba'shamayim*, our Heavenly Parent.

In recognizing the awesome privilege of having Hashem as a parent, we need to acknowledge that parents have expectations of their children that, legitimately, have to be respected. We also need to accept the fact that parents have the right, if not the obligation, to mete out "tough love" when they see their offspring moving in a direction that is self-destructive. Despite the harsh appearance that "tough love" often takes, at the core it is driven by love, the deep and uncompromising love of a parent to the well-being of their flesh and blood.

Our son Rabbi Yakov Moshe of Monsey, New York, in an address to our community, shared an on-target quip, asserting that human beings require three things for survival: food, shelter, and someone to blame.

He related that on the first day of teaching at his current position, he encountered a youngster, who, when asked his name, repeatedly and stubbornly responded, "That's a good question!" Rabbi Yakov Moshe consulted the principal, who advised him that this youngster suffered from ODD, oppositional defiance disorder. Translated into the old Yiddish vernacular, Rabbi Yakov Moshe observed, we would call it *chutzpah*. He lamented the fact that in our times, inappropriate behaviors are often excused by assigning them labels such as ADD, ADHD, CEN, OCD, PTSD, and ODD. Certainly, he qualified, there are times when these diagnoses *are* legitimate, and require empathy and professional intervention. Yet, all too often, he complained, these labels are used to absolve the individual from taking personal responsibility for their behaviors. To further aggravate the situation, America's criminal justice system has created a culture of excusing criminal behavior by assigning blame to almost everyone other than the felon. As a result, we have a society of self-proclaimed victims.

Rabbi Yakov Moshe related the Talmudic account of Rabbi Elazar ben Durdia (*Avodah Zarah* 17a), who was on a path of spiritual oblivion, having spent his life indulging in the most toxic expressions of unbridled lust and desire. On one occasion, Elazar traveled to a distant destination to avail himself of yet another carnal delight. While there, he was taunted with a stinging condemnation that he was so compromised, he was beyond *teshuvah*, repentance. Struck, suddenly, by the enormity of his transgressions, Elazar began to weep inconsolably, placing his head between his knees and crying for hours.

During this time, the Talmud relates that Elazar appealed to the mountains and the hills to plead on his behalf, and they refused. He called out to heaven and earth, to the sun and the moon, to the stars and the heavenly constellations, with no better luck. The commentaries expound that Elazar, in desperation, was trying to displace the blame on his parents; "mountains and hills" in the sacred literature represent fathers and mothers. He then sought to blame the stars, symbolic of teachers and *rebbeim*; his genetic proclivities, symbolized by the heavenly constellations, the astrological *mazalos*; and heaven and earth, Hashem's challenging providence in his life. All of them refused to give him an exit strategy, a way out.

At last, with recourse to no one, Elazar exclaimed, *"Ein ha'davar talui ela bi*—I can blame no one other than myself." With that final assumption of accountability, Elazar died, and a *bas kol*, a Heavenly echo, proclaimed, "Rabbi Elazar ben Durdia has earned entry to the World to Come."

This Talmudic Aggadah teaches us a fundamental principle of *teshuvah*; that the beginning of getting our lives back on track is taking ownership of our lapses. Only then can we truly make amends. The Ribbono Shel Olam, our Celestial Parent, who loves us dearly, expects no less of us, because He, more than anyone, knows the power that inheres in each of us. He is the one Who invested us with a majesty of being, a holy *neshamah* hewn from the Throne of Glory. Just as we have expectations of our children, wanting them to live up to their potential, so too does our Heavenly Father anguish when we don't tap into the greatness that awaits realization.

Consider the case of Ayala, a remarkable young woman, gifted with potential of a magical variety. She is brilliant, intuitive, beautiful, and extraordinarily competent and talented—in the extreme. She took an unfortunate turn at one point in her life and instead of assuming responsibility for that, she has spent years blaming others for her sad and lonely life. Her parents, siblings, and children grieve endlessly for her poor choices and the tragic waste of potential. They are all at a loss, unable to help, because in the end, Ayala alone holds the key to her healing. Her return to her true and essential self is exclusively in her hands.

We need to do our best to eliminate the "if-only's," "buts," and excuses—all the impediments to seeking the ultimate truth of our existence. We need to stop blaming others for our failures.

May Hashem, Who assures us that *"b'derech she'adam rotzeh leilech molichin oso,"* that there is Heavenly assistance to help us navigate the path we choose, bless us with the wherewithal, strength, and vision to stay the course.

Chapter 22

Perfectionism

Most people are familiar with the adage, "To them to whom much is given, much is expected." It is important to note that this adage does not conclude with the idea that *"perfection* is expected." For good reason, only G-d can deliver perfection. Human beings, with feet of clay, cannot. This does not come as a surprise to those of us who have had personal experience with a perfectionist. We know, firsthand, how terribly destructive perfectionism can be. While excellence is certainly a worthwhile goal for which to strive, the need to be perfect is clearly beyond one's reach, and consequently, an unforgiving path to pursue.

Whether we ourselves have this tendency to perfectionism, or we see it ruining the lives of our friends and loved ones, the subject needs to be recognized and addressed honestly.

My husband once expounded on the rite of the *parah adumah*, the Torah's antidote to *tumas meis*, the state of ritual restriction imposed on someone who has come in contact with a dead body. The *parah adumah* ritual involves the *shechitah* of a red heifer, an animal whose hide is perfectly red, so much so, that the presence of even two hairs of any other color disqualifies it. After its slaughter, the animal is set to fire, and its ashes are sprinkled upon the *tamei* person as part of an elaborate purification process.

My husband commented that the heifer's requisite for consummate redness corresponds to people's pathological preoccupation with perfection. Since perfection is rarely, if ever, attainable, perfectionists often refrain from investing in any worthwhile pursuit for fear of not being able to execute it faultlessly. In doing so, they stifle the potential that might otherwise legitimately be realized. This loss of potential is tantamount to death, which renders a person *tamei*. The slaughtering and burning of the "perfectly" red heifer makes the statement that perfectionism must be excised if one is to counteract the "contamination" to which it leads.

Some time ago, I was introduced to Daniella, a young wife and mother who was the apple of her parents' eyes. The sun rose and set on this youngest of their children, who, as far as her parents were concerned, could do no wrong. Everything she achieved was celebrated in superlatives. Daniella grew up, married well, and set up house. Her parents' exaggerated high opinion of her shaped her perception of herself to the point that nothing less than perfection was an option for her. She felt pressured to be the perfect wife, mother, housekeeper, and professional. Predictably, nothing Daniella did ever quite hit the mark. Her standards were unrealistic and over the top.

She once commented to me that we all have a prosecutor in our heads who points out the things we have done wrong, but no defense attorney to protect us. Daniella constantly beat herself up over the house not being spotless, the laundry not always being done in a timely fashion, the meals not being fancy enough, and the children not immaculately dressed. The inner critic in her head would not let up. Her insatiable and unattainable need for perfection eventually caused Daniella serious health issues. Her health professionals diagnosed her condition as one directly related to the unreal and unrelenting demands she made on herself. Upon their recommendation, Daniella sought therapeutic intervention and came to understand that her perfectionism was driven by an insecure ego that craved the approval of others to shore up her own lack of self- esteem.

Eventually, Daniella came to the point where she no longer became unhinged if someone walked through the door and saw a less than immaculate home. She was able to host guests without driving herself crazy for weeks in advance. As a result, her health improved. She personified the observation that "calm is a great power"—a calm that is the product of knowing that one is required to put forth no more than their best effort. Daniella began to exude the power of calm, and everyone around her benefitted tremendously.

Do you recognize a little of this tendency in yourself? In a friend?

Interestingly, the obsession to excel is referenced by our Sages in a Talmudic comment (*Bava Metzia* 87a) going back thousands of years. In the beginning of *Parashas Vayeira*, the text describes the visit of three Heavenly angels, who appear to Avraham and Sarah as ordinary wayfarers. Avraham, the consummate host, hurries to request of Sarah that she bake breads of *"kemach solles"* for the guests. Since *kemach* and *solles* both mean flour, our Sages are moved to reflect on the redundancy. The commentaries understand the Talmudic resolution to explain that Avraham said *"kemach,"* referring to a coarser flour, whereas Sarah insisted on *"solles,"* the finest flour.

Our Sages conclude: *"Mi'kan she'ha'ishah tzarah eineha b'orchim yoser min ha'ish*—From here we derive that a woman is less inclined to receive guests eagerly than a man." The explanation for this conclusion is based on the fact that if a woman feels that she must offer only *solles,* i.e., the very finest and best, her eagerness to welcome guests will be limited by the effort that it requires. Indeed, the Torah wants us to know that though we might think that more and bigger is better, we have to ask if, at the core, it is perfectionism that is driving the effort. If so, it is destined to be counterproductive and ultimately to implode.

The classic Chassidic commentary, the *Meor Einayim*, explains that Moshe Rabbeinu is described as having reached the greatest level of understanding of the Divine known to man, fifty levels of *binah*, minus one. The *Meor Einayim* says that the "minus one" is the recognition that as a human being, one cannot achieve everything, and that accepting the truth of "minus one" is the highest level. Someone commented wisely that only imperfect people can move us toward a perfect world.

May Hashem give us the wisdom to strive for our personal excellence, without the pressure of having to be perfect. That willingness to accept the imperfection of ourselves and our friends is...well...perfect.

Chapter 23

Seeing Ourselves and Others

Sinas chinam, hating someone for no good reason, is often cited as the root cause of many tragedies that our nation has suffered through its history. According to one of the commentators, the reason the Jewish People strayed from Torah observance, thereby invoking the Divine wrath, was due to the deep-rooted feeling within that whispered in our ears that we were *chinam*—inadequate, unworthy, and *nothing*—and that, therefore, whatever we did was ultimately of little, if any, value.

This began with the episode of the *Meraglim*, the spies sent to scout out Eretz Yisrael, whose negative reports discouraged the nation and brought them to tears over the loss of their dream. At the core of their grief was the conviction that they were *chinam*, unworthy and incapable of fighting for and conquering the Land.

The *bechiyah shel chinam*, crying over nothing, was in fact a crying over their own *nothingness*—a tragic misperception that has challenged us through the ages as we tried to recover our faith and self-confidence. This recovery is only achievable when we recognize that if we are connected to the Ribbono Shel Olam, our Source, then absolutely everything—even conquering powerful enemies, both external and internal—is totally doable.

Not surprisingly, when an attitude of *chinam* prevails, it invariably brings with it *sinas chinam*, hatred of others for no good reason. This hatred feeds on the hatred of *oneself*, of struggling with the feeling of *chinam*, of the "nothingness," within ourselves. We are bedeviled by a black hole inside of our psyche that drives us to make ourselves feel better by disparaging others. Sadly, we have paid a huge price for this indiscretion throughout the centuries, with all of our national catastrophes. Alas, we have been subjected to what feels like a never-ending *galus*.

The antidote to feelings of *chinam* is to recognize that our worth emanates from the Ribbono Shel Olam's investiture of a *neshamah* in each and every one of us, the *"pintele Yid,"* which is inextinguishable and incorruptible. An apt metaphor given is that of a light bulb, ready and prepared with all its wiring in place, and all we have to do is turn on the switch. Our exalted *neshamos* are wired for great things. The caveat is that it is up to each of us to activate the mechanism by recognizing the potential that exists in us and flipping the switch.

The absence of self-worth manifests itself in a myriad of ways:

- Daniel, a very presentable and intelligent young man, masked his inner turmoil very well. However, when it came to finding a suitable mate, it surfaced in his insistence on "tall and gorgeous." Tall and gorgeous happened, but, predictably, it did not last very long. In the many conversations we had, it became clear that Daniel needed a "trophy wife," to prove to himself and others that he was a "something." Daniel eventually realized that counteracting his deeply ingrained feelings of nothingness by superficial modalities was not only counterproductive but was actually contributing to his failure. His growing resolve to alter the dynamics of his existence is a work in progress, as he becomes more and more aware of the fact that his relationships and choices have to reflect the inner strength waiting to be tapped. Indeed, "the switch that has to be turned on."

- Ruthie is another case in point. Ruthie came to one of our teaching weekends dressed very inappropriately. After a number of encounters, it became clear that Ruthie was a young woman with much to offer—goodness, intelligence, and a quest for knowledge. The way she presented herself was all the more mystifying, because she actually came from a *heimishe* background and certainly knew better. I liked Ruthie, and because I developed a great affinity for her, she ultimately opened up to me and shared that she came from a large family, where, as she put it, she "fell between the cracks." Unfortunately, Ruthie felt that since she was already a disappointment to her family, she might as well subscribe to a different set of values. I suggested to Ruthie that her inappropriate appearance was a statement. She was basically projecting the message, "Look at me. This is the sum total of who I am." Her subconscious agenda was to put people off. Her fear was that if someone came too close to her, they would discover the real her, and being the self-deprecating person that she was, she could not chance that someone would discover how worthless she was. Perceiving herself as *chinam*, as damaged goods, Ruthie put up walls, her inappropriate dress being one of them. As such, she could keep people at arm's length. Her wounded psyche could not risk closeness with others. Ruthie wept as she acknowledged my assessment. Again, feelings of *chinam* propel us to strange places, very distant from our essence.

- Perhaps one of the most tragic examples was that of Hershel. Hershel was unquestionably one of the most brilliant and talented people I have ever met. Anyone who has met him would have predicted a great future for him. In reality, Hershel has—for the last forty years—been "stuck." He has consistently rejected opportunity after opportunity for suitable employment by focusing on the negative in every situation. Hershel sought guarantees. He was terrified at the possibility of failure. Clearly, Hershel's fear was that failure would confirm his deeply rooted feelings of *chinam*, of inadequacy, and his fragile ego could not handle that possibility.

- An inspiring example of someone who against all odds would not allow the phenomenon of *chinam* to invade and take over her person was Miriam. Nobody would have ever imagined that given Miriam's positive affect, comportment, and admirable achievements, her formative years had been an unimaginable nightmare. Orphaned at birth, Miriam was raised in an abusive foster home. She was never given a free pass in life. Despite the attempts of her many caretakers to marginalize her, Miriam held on tightly to her sense of self. She refused to live in the dark and debilitating space of *chinam*. Remarkably, she did indeed find the light switch, and has moved on to marry and build a beautiful family.

Someone aptly observed that the definition of courage is moving forward despite fear. The courage we require is unquestionably a product of tapping into the best part of ourselves that, oftentimes, we don't believe exists. And, if on occasion we do "fail," as inevitably we all do, it is simply an invitation to persevere, to regroup, and to go back into the "ring" and flex our spiritual and emotional muscles, with ever greater determination.

The beginning of it all is to cease looking at ourselves—and others—as *chinam*. The beginning of it all is to look at others—and ourselves—as infinitely valuable and unique.

PART IV

MINDFULNESS

Chapter 24

Little Problems, Big Problems

A wise person once observed that life is by nature a series of small problems. Only, he concluded, if one is struck by a single large problem should there be cause for concern.

One such "large" problem occurred some time ago when I began having incidents of unexplained high fever that came on suddenly at random intervals. To make matters worse, my ordinarily elevated blood pressure tanked erratically, leaving me trembling and shaking uncontrollably. The first two such attacks occurred when we were trying to grab some "R and R" in Palm Springs, California, and landed me in two separate urgent care facilities. Despite the severity of the symptoms and numerous tests, they were unable to come up with a diagnosis.

The next two attacks occurred upon my return to Milwaukee, whereupon my physician hospitalized me for sustained periods in an effort to determine what was happening. Top specialists in every field were brought on board to unravel the mystery, and I was subjected to a barrage of tests and diagnostic procedures that I never knew existed and couldn't spell. After endless tests and scans, the medical community concluded that I was an "enigma." As of this writing, they still do not have a diagnosis. *Baruch Hashem*, I have not had an episode since my last dismissal from the hospital, and I am guardedly hopeful that the worst is over.

Lest I feel too sorry for myself, my granddaughter Ruchel called to tell me that her seven-year-old, Shabse, was suffering as well. He had come home from cheder grinning from ear to ear with his new Chumash in tow. Shabse ran into the kitchen to share his great prize with his mother. Predictably, she was delighted, but proceeded absentmindedly to put the Chumash down on the kitchen counter where in no time at all it was sopping wet. Though crushed, Shabsi accepted his mother's assurance that it would be dry by the next day. The following day, Shabse came home with a new *machberes*, a new notebook. Again, he showed it off to his mother, who once again absentmindedly placed it near the sink where it suffered the same fate as his Chumash. Little Shabse could no longer contain himself, and he cried out, "First my Chumash, now my *machberes*, my whole life is wet!"

And here I thought I had problems. Shortly thereafter, Ruchel called again to tell me that her four-year-old, Surah'le, a little pistol of a child, had approached her in great frustration, and with a stomping of her feet had declared that it was taking way too long for her to grow up.

A four-year-old's impatience with time that is moving too slowly is humorous and evokes chuckles. But what about us adults? Indeed, how often have we wished precious time away. Too many of us have commented, on occasion, that we would like to see ourselves on the other side of a wedding, a bar mitzvah, or a Yom Tov. This attitude, while understandable, is unquestionably an unfortunate one, because every moment of life should be relished. Those of us who have been around the block a few times appreciate the fact that it takes only a blink of the eye to realize that time has gone by way too quickly, and with it, important parts of the familiar landscape that was so precious to us.

The midrash states that "the currency of Moshe Rabbeinu was *az* [i.e., just then]"—in other words, the ability to be in the moment. The understanding is that at every juncture of Moshe Rabbeinu's life, he was fully present. One such example was "**Az** *yashir Moshe*—**Then** Moshe sang," referring to B'nei Yisrael's salvation with the miraculous splitting of the sea. One might have assumed that Moshe Rabbeinu would be distracted by the many upcoming practical concerns of catering to a nation of millions of people in the desert—how would he feed them, supply them with water, and protect them from the desert heat and the poisonous snakes and scorpions that swarmed the desert wilderness? Such, however, was not the case. Moshe Rabbeinu was totally engaged in the celebration of the moment, the great event at hand. Neither concerns of the past nor those of the future robbed him of his exquisite mindfulness of being in *az*, the present moment.

Certainly, none of us can achieve the level of a Moshe Rabbeinu. Yet, the lesson he modeled for us is one to which we should all aspire in some appreciable measure. "Life in the playpen," as experienced by seven-year-old Shabse and four-year-old Sura'le, is one that hopefully, as adults, we have outgrown. The litmus test is often in the area of relationships. Are we fully present when our friends and loved ones need us? Are we fully present when they unburden themselves to us?

Chapter 25
Listening

A woman approached me recently after I had concluded a lecture out of town and asked for a *berachah*. Although it is not my wont to give *berachos*, I responded that I would be happy to confer upon her a heartfelt *berachah*, for whatever it was worth, and to include her in my *tefillos*. I asked what kind of *berachah* she needed.

She replied that she needed a blessing for a *refuah sheleimah* and good health. She explained that some years earlier she had been diagnosed with brain cancer and that it had recently resurfaced. The woman must have sensed my incredulity at her cheerful demeanor, and she shared her story.

She said that the first time around, the illness had rendered her unable to speak for months. At first, she was terribly frustrated and angry at the injustice of it all. After a while, however, she realized that for the first time in her life she was being forced to *listen*. She confessed that this was eye-opening for her. Previously, she hadn't really heard people out. She would often interrupt them on the assumption that she knew what they were going to say. When she lost the ability to speak, she had no choice but to pay attention.

The result was that people began to feel comfortable talking to her intimately, revealing themselves in a deeper way; they knew they were being fully heard even though she could do no more than nod in response. She learned something valuable from this experience, painful though it was.

The art of listening is barely in evidence in our culture. We are in such a hurry to say our piece that others, especially our significant others, feel marginalized.

A story is told in the name of Rav Shalom Schwadron, the renowned Maggid of Yerushalayim, about a motorist who had a flat tire in front of a psychiatric hospital that was enclosed by an imposing fence. The motorist took out his spare tire and began to remove the flat, inserting the bolts he had removed into the hubcap. Suddenly, a passing car struck the hubcap and sent it and the bolts flying in all directions.

The man searched but was unable to locate all the missing bolts, without which he could not put on the spare. As he stood there wondering what to do, a resident of the hospital who had been watching from behind the fence asked if he could help. After hesitating for a moment, the motorist explained his dilemma, and the patient offered a very practical and simple solution; he suggested that the motorist remove one bolt from each of the three remaining tires and use them to secure the spare. Although this solution was less than ideal, it would suffice until the motorist could get to an auto supply store.

The motorist was astonished by the ingenuity of this simple idea and wondered how a seriously compromised person could have come up with it. Sensing his unspoken question, the resident sighed and remarked, "We are not here because we are stupid; we are here because we are not well. The difference between us and the rest of the world is that in many instances we are offered help that could relieve us of our torment and pain, but we are unable to listen and process what we hear."

It is commonly understood that mental health is a spectrum. To some extent, each person responds to the unhealthy voices within, at the same time listening respectfully to the realities without and yielding to their logic. When one is overwhelmed by strident inner demands, to the point where counsel from the world of practicality is obstructed, pathology has made an inroad. One sign of healthy functioning is the ability to set aside personal convictions of infallibility and to respect the fact that others may have something valuable to say. In short, to be able to listen deeply is a mark of true well-being.

In *Tehillim* 17:1, David HaMelech uses three expressions to denote listening: *ha'azin, hakshiv,* and *shema.* The commentaries explain that these represent three levels of listening:

1. *Ha'azin* refers to the basic auditory function of hearing.
2. *Hakshiv* refers to a higher level of paying attention.
3. *Shema* refers to listening with one's heart and soul.

These levels are relevant both in our exchanges with Hashem and in our interactions with people. At different times, we listen with different degrees of attention.

Healthy human relationships—our connections to friends and family—are heavily dependent on our ability to fine-tune our listening skills, listening not only to the words uttered but to what is behind them. This requires us to approach others with an open mind.

Similarly, as David HaMelech shows us, the key to our relationship with our Heavenly Father is found in the expression "*Shema Yisrael*—Hear O Israel"; we are asked to pay attention, to listen, and to hear on a deep level, allowing the words to penetrate our very being. It has always been Klal Yisrael's fervent hope and prayer that we will learn to listen, thereby meriting to hear the shofar of *Mashiach Tzidkeinu,* speedily in our time.

Chapter 26

Being Present

The reality is that if we move through life consciously, and mindfully, we can glean spiritual messages from the most unlikely sources.

I had to chuckle when Nicky, my non-Jewish physical therapist, in an attempt to help me remember how to climb stairs effectively after my hip surgery, gave me the following tips: "When going *up*, use your *good* leg, as everyone knows the *good* ultimately go *up* to Heaven. When going *down*, go with your *bad* leg, which reminds us of the *bad*, who go *down* to you-know-where." Navigating and climbing steps has never been the same since Nicky apprised me of my spiritual options.

Another humorous lesson came to me when our son, Rabbi Mordechai, of London, England, told me that his precious daughters are afraid of missing out on any tidbits of the latest news in town. In the current vernacular, this is referred to as "FOMO," the fear of missing out. They would therefore follow their mother, Rivka'lah, around the house wherever she went when she was talking on the phone. On one occasion, Rivka'lah, frustrated by the lack of privacy, turned to them in frustration and admonished them for being so intrusive. Bruchy, their ten-year-old, smiled and said, "Mommy, we are doing what you always told us you wanted, we are following in your footsteps!" Indeed, isn't that what we all want of our children?

It is well-known that hairdressers, and, by extension, *sheitel machers* (wig stylists) are therapists in disguise. Stressed and exhausted women come into their studios, plop themselves down into the chairs—which for them become the veritable psychiatrist's couch—and both literally and figuratively "let their hair down." A *sheitel* appointment becomes a welcome opportunity for women to unburden themselves of the many stresses in their lives and get a new perspective on their troubles.

I first became aware of this phenomenon when visiting my daughter Bas Sheva, who, until her recent move to Lakewood, serviced *sheitels* in Yerushalayim for eight years. During our visits in Israel, women everywhere would approach me and tell me that besides her talented work, she is such a bright and caring person. They claimed that her demeanor was so empathic and approachable that they felt safe sharing their problems and seeking advice for many of their issues. Ironically, I have not been the beneficiary of my daughter's expertise, because I don't wear human-hair sheitels, which are exclusively Bas Sheva's forte.

I am, however, fortunate to have Rochel Newman, a dear friend and extraordinarily talented *sheitel macher*, who, as Bas Sheva puts it, "has hands that move in a magical way." Recently, when I arrived for my appointment, Rochel was talking with utmost patience and compassion with an elderly customer who seemed to be fragile of both mind and body. Rochel was helping her plan her trip home with *sheitel* boxes in tow. With kindness and obvious caring, she urged the elderly lady to take a taxi, rather than venture out on public transportation. The woman was not easily convinced, but Rochel persevered until she acceded. Rochel then took the woman's boxes, walked her to the elevator and escorted her down three floors to a waiting cab. This was certainly way beyond the call of duty. Rochel is irrefutable proof that even New Yorkers, who are not popularly identified with tenderhearted and chivalrous behavior, can be exemplary human beings. There is no doubt that whatever our field of endeavor may be, there are always opportunities to go the extra mile, to be sensitive, to extend kindness, to soothe, to comfort, and to uplift and enrich another person's life.

Counterintuitive as it may be, even those who have been injured by life, who have had what they refer to as "misery training," can transform their painful experiences for the sake of helping others.

To that effect, I found in my notes a quote from Sheila Nevin, who writes:

> *I loved my mother, but at the same time resented her. I lived in a private, war-torn universe. I lived with a noose around my neck, and so I became me. People talk of moments that make you change, that determine who you are. That moment was mine. I would realize that I understood people and their suffering and somewhere in that understanding was a place for me. I chose to share and tell the stories of the struggle to triumph in an uncertain and often cruel world.*

Sheila has devoted her life to serving as a resource for others, who like herself were similarly traumatized by their childhood experiences. The point is that rather than cursing the darkness and living her life as a victim of the past, Sheila has, as the cliché states, taken lemons and made lemonade. We all benefit from the Sheilas of the world who refuse to allow the painful imprints of their formative years to define them in a negative way. Their refusal to surrender and go "silently into the dark night" of defeat is an inspiration to everyone to stay the course.

No less so are the Bas Shevas and the Rochels of the world, who are the extraordinary, ordinary people that do remarkable things—and raise the bar for all of us. We can all be motivated by their example.

The messages and lessons are always present. The question is whether or not we will be "present" enough to get the message. Investing mindfulness into our days would help us realize that no matter who we are, where we are, or what we do, there is an implicit invitation to stop, look, hear, and notice the legion lessons that flow to us from virtually every precinct in our lives.

In addition, we also become increasingly aware of our fellow human beings, their needs and challenges, and become enriched by enriching others. What are your friends telling you, without words? That is usually the most important part of the conversation—the part that reveals what they truly need.

Living mindfully opens expansive horizons of opportunities to grow in mind, heart, and spirit. It's never too late to begin.

Chapter 27
Experiencing the Now

L ast Shavuos, aside from the many spectacular Torah sessions and inspiring insights I was privileged to hear, there was an experiential moment that I found particularly instructive.

My daughter Bas Sheva and her family came from Lakewood to spend the Yom Tov with us. In a desire to enjoy their stay, fleeting as I knew it would be, I took time out of my hectic schedule to take the grandchildren for a walk. Nine-year-old Sarah, seven-year-old Avrumi, and three-year-old Yankele accompanied me.

As we began walking, I cut short the chattering by commenting to Avrumi that when we returned to the house, we needed to groom his *peyos* and brush Sarah's hair. Wise beyond his years, Avrumi, a miniature philosopher, responded to me, "Bubbi, we are now taking a walk. Think about the walk—the blue sky, the pretty flowers, and the green grass. Now," he continued, "is not the time to think about messy hair and *peyos*. All that will have to be taken care of later."

I couldn't believe what I was hearing. It was like a message from Heaven exhorting me to stop in my tracks, slow the wheels of the mad,

mad world, take notice, and be present in the moment; a moment that will inevitably pass all too quickly.

Shortly before that conversation, local events confirmed the crucial necessity of being "present," of celebrating what we have, both personally and communally. Mr. Todd Miller, a pillar of our *kehillah*, died in a tragic car accident at the young age of sixty-one, leaving behind a widow and seven adult children and their families. He was here one moment, vibrant and attending to the needs of both individuals and virtually every major Torah institution in the city, and then, shockingly, he was gone the next. The community was thrown into a state of disbelief and mourning.

Todd's sudden disappearance amplified the message that little Avrumi was bringing to my attention. The unpleasant reality is that we never know what the next moment will bring. It behooves us, consequently, to be careful not to leave loose ends, to regularly ask ourselves the sobering question that if life were, *chas v'shalom*, to end unexpectedly for oneself or a loved one, what would we have wanted to have said or done. Most often, people regret having been so distracted with the frenzy of life that they put their friends and loved ones—and the attention they should be giving them—on the back burner. We genuinely expect to tend to them, but *not right now*. We say to ourselves that there are more immediate and pressing issues that require our attention. At this moment, our friends and family are not our priority. What a devastating price this may potentially exact going forward.

Seven-year-old Avrumi echoed that same thought this week, by pointing out that our hassled existence should not keep us from seeing what is front and center in our lives, be it a beautiful spring day, the smile of a friend, or the expression of love from and toward the significant others in our lives.

PART V

UNITY

Chapter 28
The Secret of the Jew

In his book, *The Secret of the Jews*, David Ben Moshe documents the comments of many prominent non-Jews, among them virulent anti-Semites who are at a loss to explain "the secret of the Jew." Among others, he quotes Mark Twain, who famously said:

> *The Egyptian, the Babylonian, and the Persian rose, filled the planet with sound and splendor, then faded to dream-stuff and passed away; the Greek and the Roman followed; and made a vast noise, and they are gone; other people have sprung up and held their torch high for a time, but it burned out, and they sit in twilight now, or have vanished. The Jew saw them all, beat them all, and is now what he always was, exhibiting no decadence, no infirmities of age, no weakening of his parts, no slowing of his energies, no dulling of his alert and aggressive mind. All things are mortal but the Jew; all other forces pass, but he remains. What is the secret of his immortality?*

Indeed, what is our secret?

Every year on Purim we annually celebrate the miracle of vanquishing Haman, an Amalekite descendant, who came frighteningly close to carrying out his plan to annihilate the Jewish People. The miracle of Purim celebrates our salvation—another example of the "immortality of the Jew"—as well as the role that Jews played in this phenomenon. Clearly, at that time, we, as a nation, had lost our way. Our Sages describe widespread assimilation into a society that was eager to embrace us. In frightening similarity to our own times, too many Jews succumbed to the blandishments of the seductive Persian culture, making accommodations that progressively eroded their Jewish identity. Only a modest number, Mordechai and Esther among them, were not blindsided, and remained completely faithful to their heritage. With imminent destruction looming over the heads of the nation, Mordechai and Esther rallied the people to fast, pray, and recommit to the sacred values of the Torah. The external miracle, represented by the defeat of Haman and his sympathizers throughout the kingdom, began, as it always has, with an internal "miracle," that of the return of Hashem's people to the observance of His Will.

One of the unique features of the Purim events was the way in which Hashem's *hashgachah pratis* (Divine providence) orchestrated events quietly, under the cover of nature. Only in retrospect was His Hand in the circumstances leading to Klal Yisrael's ultimate victory, explicit and transparent.

In reality, hidden miracles occur daily in our lives, quietly, unbeknown and undetected by most. One such heartwarming story occurred in our community and speaks volumes to the factors that invite miracles into our lives.

David and Meyer and their wives are treasured members of our community. They had both been married for a number of years without being blessed with children. It is well-known that being called up for the *aliyah* of *Kol Hane'arim* on Simchas Torah, when all the little children gather under a tallis to collectively recite the *berachah* over the Torah, is a *segulah* for having children.

Learning of this *segulah*, David put in a bid for this special *aliyah*, in the hope that in its merit he would be granted a child. Unbeknown to

David, at the same time, Meyer approached the gabbai with the very same request, having the identical purpose in mind. When David found out that Meyer had put in his request, he went to the gabbai and insisted that his own bid be dismissed, and that Meyer should be granted the *aliyah*. Providentially, when Meyer became aware of David's wish, he argued that David, who had been married longer than himself, should have priority. Finally, David and Meyer confronted each other, each insisting that the other should be given the *aliyah*.

Observing the scene, our son Rabbi Benzion assured Meyer that his magnificent act of deference would certainly be as precious to the Ribbono Shel Olam as the actual *aliyah*, and undoubtedly, they would both be blessed.

Indeed, incredibly, *both* David and Meyer's wives were quickly blessed with baby boys. Miracles? Certainly, but ones that were inspired by their own deeds, their caring, concern, and deference to each other.

The story of Meyer and David is strongly reminiscent of a story of unknown origin about two brothers who worked their respective fields, on opposite sides of a mountain, with diligence. One year, the crop was particularly bountiful. One brother, who had no children, decided to take a portion of his produce and surreptitiously place it in his brother's silo in the middle of the night, since his brother had a large family and needed the produce more than he did. In the quiet of the night, he scaled the mountain to carry out his loving intent. At the same time, his married brother concluded that the single brother could use more produce since he had no children to take care of him in his old age and would therefore need more personal resources. He, too, waited until dark to climb the mountain to deposit his heartfelt gift to his brother. This happened several nights in succession until one night, midway, the two brothers met with bundles of wheat in tow. They were so touched by their mutual concern, that they fell upon each other's necks and cried tears of love and gratitude. Legend has it that Hashem, looking down from Heaven, decided there and then that this place where brothers met in such devotion to each other would be the appropriate place to establish His eternal home, the Beis Hamikdash.

Speaking of Purim, we can glean a powerful lesson from Purim that should affect us throughout the year. The miracle of Purim is celebrated with *matanos l'evyonim*, gifts to the poor, and with *mishloach manos ish l're'eihu*, gifts of food sent to one's friends.

The message is loud and clear. Hashem's miraculous intervention is most propitious when we are lovingly inclusive of all of our brethren. Of all the many reasons Hashem has shown His Hand in history, our coming together in *achdus*, unity, is beyond a doubt one of the most powerful determinants. Above all else, our sacred literature asserts, this component is essential to "the immortality of the Jew."

Chapter 29

Our Trip

W̶e had spent four weeks in Eretz Yisrael, and because of our busy schedule, I had yet to visit two of Eretz Yisrael's holiest sites, Kever Rachel and the Kosel. On our last day there, my good friend Sarah volunteered to drive me to these *mekomos ha'kedoshim*. Despite the need to pack and get ready for our journey back to the States, I eagerly accepted. It was a glorious day, with skies the color blue that one only beholds in Eretz Yisrael. As the Kosel came into view, the sun played its magic on the sacred stones so that even at a distance, they glowed with an otherworldly brightness that cast its spell on me. Predictably, as we approached the Kosel, we found friends from all over the globe, who, like ourselves, were making this singular pilgrimage. As always, the massive stones were cool and soothing to the touch. I couldn't help but wonder how these stones, despite their formidable size and density, were able to withstand the ocean of tears shed over thousands of years by all the heavy hearts that poured their woes out in front of them. Every corner, nook, and cranny, full of *k'vitlach*, gave testimony to the heart-wrenching pleas of so many desperate souls.

Many years ago, Benny Levy, a young man who came to Milwaukee as a *shaliach* from Israel to teach youngsters in the Diaspora would sit at our Shabbos table and sing a song entitled "The Kotel."

The refrain was *"Yesh anashim im lev shel even, yesh avanim im lev shel adam*—There are people with hearts of stone, and there are stones with a heart."

Inside the tunnel wall, we came upon a group of women who invited us to join them in the recitation of *Nishmas*. These were women of all backgrounds, some sporting *tichlach*, others *sheitels*, and others less observant, all lifting their voices together in praise of the One and Only Ribbono Shel Olam. Additionally, it was fascinating to see that upon taking leave of the Kosel, every one of them—even those who appeared less connected to observance—reverently backed out, facing the wall, rather than turning their backs to it. Reverence for this holy place is manifest everywhere, and lost on no one. I was overcome by the realization that sacred as the Kosel is, it is only a wall, a small remnant of the majestic house of G-d that graced our lives in the past.

From there we proceeded to Kever Rachel, the time-honored resting place of the matriarch Rachel. The verse in *Yirmiyahu* states: "Rachel is crying for her children and refuses to be comforted." When you close your eyes there, you can almost hear Rachel's cry—and Hashem's reassurance to her that "He will return them to their boundaries." Hashem promises that B'nei Yisrael from everywhere—Rachel's precious progeny—will come home.

The overwhelming feeling that lingered in the wake of our trip was the urgency to gather all of our people and go "home." Almost as a postscript, on our way back to America, we flew with a different carrier then El Al, the airline that had brought us to Israel. I couldn't help but react to the contrast in languages between the two airlines in all the announcements during the flight. One was our own historic tongue, albeit with some contemporary modifications, while the other brought back some painful memories.

For all Jews, it is important to underscore the fact that Israel is not only a geographic place, but a religious identity. Our daughter Chana Malka called to share one such illustration. Esther, a young woman in her husband's *beis midrash*, has, of late, become very close to Rebbetzin Rochel Singer of Alexander, Chana Malka's mother-in-law. Esther joins the Rebbetzin periodically for the Shabbos *seudos*. Rebbetzin Singer related to Chana Malka that Esther recently took a trip to Israel and returned to the US on Turkish Airlines. Esther and another woman seemed to be the only Jews on the flight. The two of them, though they had not known each other before, stayed together, both feeling lost and somewhat anxious as they landed in Istanbul. As they roamed the airport waiting for their connecting flight to America, a young Chassidic fellow came over to them and asked them if they needed to use his cell phone, or if there was anything else he could do for them. In addition, he insisted on helping them with their luggage, dragging it to the next gate. Although they were apprehensive at first and suspicious about his offers to help, they realized that he had no agenda other than to be helpful to fellow Jews, and they were delighted with this "angel" that Hashem had sent them. As he took leave, they asked him for his name. He responded that his name was Yitzchok Fox, that he lived in Milwaukee, Wisconsin, and that he was a member of the Twerski community. Upon hearing this story, the venerable Rebbetzin Singer exclaimed, "Only from Milwaukee can one expect behavior like this. Only from Milwaukee!" Needless to say, our daughter Chana Malka, who has suffered over the years from in-towners disparaging her "small" hometown, was delighted. She felt proud and vindicated. It didn't hurt that she had scored points with her beloved mother-in-law, who is my dear and much esteemed *machetenesta*. Chana Malka's conclusion was that Rabbi Yitzchok Fox had made not only a *kiddush Hashem*, but also a "*kiddush Milwaukee*."

All in all, expressions of love and caring for each other among our people will hasten the fulfillment of Hashem's promise to "Mama Rochel," that He will send Mashiach to gather us in and take us back home. As we draw close to Purim, it is a propitious time to close ranks and work on our *ahavas Yisrael*. That will most certainly convince our Maker that the time to make good on His promise has come.

Chapter 30
Ambiguous Grief

Contemporary psychologists identify an emotional phenomenon they call "ambiguous grief." Ambiguous grief describes a state of anguish that, rather than being associated with death, attaches itself to situations that are unnecessarily invested with extraordinary heartache.

One such situation involves the tragic splintering of families. While the fracturing of families is deplorable wherever it occurs, it is especially so when it happens among Hashem's elect people, Klal Yisrael. Indeed, the Torah was only given to us in the desert when the Jewish People came together "*k'ish echad b'lev echad*—as one person with one heart." Our Sages teach that only when everyone renounced their personal agendas and annoyances and came together as a single loving, caring family did we earn the right to a revelation of Hashem's will. Yet, time and again, in macrocosm and microcosm, we—who should know better—allow our precious *achdus*, our precious unity, to be compromised by strife and animosity.

In recent memory, the internal squabbles of prominent families, as well as painful institutional frictions that caused discord in the leadership of Chassidic followings and yeshiva faculties, have caused inordinate hurt and suffering to our communities. In the instance of public conflict, the pain is manifold. It is all the more unfortunate because the protagonists in these disputes are ones to whom we look as models to emulate.

Over the years I have had occasion to counsel families in crisis, where well-intentioned parents found themselves dealing with angry children whose bickering and jealousies were destroying the fabric of the family. It is my experience that there is practically no greater pain for parents than to find themselves accused of not being fair and evenhanded in their relationship with their children.

Psychologists note that at the core of most personal or professional dissension is the need to "win." It seems that all human beings have an innate desire to triumph. Winning boosts one's sense of self and worth. The *sefarim ha'kedoshim* teach that the attribute of *netzach* is a Divinely endowed characteristic related to "winning," which G-d intended us to use in our battles with our *yetzer hara*. However, instead of using this need to win in the battles for our eternity, we too often mistakenly strive for temporal victories and acquisitions.

In *Sefer Tehillim*, David HaMelech advises us that "there is nothing more beautiful and pleasant than brothers dwelling together in unity." Our Sages amplify this, saying that "there is no vessel that can contain and sustain blessings other than peace." What derails us repeatedly is our ability to rationalize our positions. Indeed, personal agendas hijack our clear thinking and sensitivities. What should give us pause is that it has long been established and verified that the less we have on the inside, the more we need on the outside, and therefore, the greater our need to "win".

An anecdote is told of two neighbors who came to the rabbi seeking mediation over a strip of land between their respective properties that each claimed belonged to them. Seeing how vehement and impassioned they were, the rabbi asked them to take him to the contested site. Once there, the rabbi prostrated himself with his ear to the ground, asking the land to reveal who was its rightful inheritor. After a few moments, he lifted his head and declared, "The land asserts that it belongs to neither of you. Rather, both of you, it says, belong to it."

The significance of maintaining perspective was driven home to me many years ago when a precious family heirloom that had been designated for my husband by his father was claimed by another, more distant family member. My children, all of whom knew that it was meant for their father, were predictably irate. My husband's memorable response to them was that his father's memory and those of his ancestors would certainly not be honored if he were to engage in a tug-of-war that would divide the family. His wise counsel was to let it go, maintaining the peace with those in this world and giving *nachas* to those in the world beyond.

At the end of the day, it is not things, glory, or turf that we take with us. It is, curiously, our ability to "lose," especially in those areas that are fleeting, so that we can "win" in the realm that is everlasting.

Chapter 31
One Soul

The heinous murders of eleven Jews at prayer in Pittsburgh, Pennsylvania, in October 2018, evoked intense grief and anguish from B'nei Yisrael around the globe. Understandably, Jewish communities in America were most affected, and communal gatherings to try and process the sadness and outrage were held in cities throughout the United States. Milwaukee was no exception to this rule, and the Torah community, including the *yungeleit* of the Milwaukee Kollel and the *talmidim* of our local Chofetz Chaim Yeshiva (WITS), joined to hear words of *chizuk* from their spiritual leaders. The event affected me deeply.

The first to address a packed assemblage was Rabbi Avrohom Boruch Rauch, the Rosh Yeshiva of WITS. Rabbi Rauch noted that just as Tishah B'Av, which commemorates the day our two *Batei Hamikdash* were destroyed thousands of years ago, is still mourned every year by Jews in every corner of the globe, so too is the death of every individual Jew a tragedy for all Jews wherever they live and for all of time. He eloquently expanded on the theme of Jewish unity and explained how an assault on one Jew is an assault on all Jews. Only in acknowledging and deepening our *achdus*, our eternal oneness, can we merit to overcome our enemies.

Rabbi Mendel Senderovic, our Rosh Kollel, began his remarks by saying that a human being cannot possibly explain a single death, let alone a calamity such as what happened in Pittsburgh. He noted that he was the child of survivors who had lost many loved ones during the terrible Holocaust years, including his own siblings. He said that to their great credit, his parents did not adopt a fatalistic attitude to life. Instead, they deliberately and purposefully set about rebuilding their lives with a positive and joyful attitude. Their response to tragedy was that Jews don't succumb to intimidation. Rather, just as our nation has from time immemorial demonstrated that in the face of tragedy, we pull ourselves up and embrace life with resilience, so too would they. Rabbi Senderovic called on us to resist fear and intimidation and move forward resolutely to fortify our Jewish identity with joy and determination.

My husband was the concluding speaker. He elaborated on Rabbi Rauch's theme of *achdus* by referencing a classic explanation by the Lubliner Rav, Rabbi Meir Shapiro, on Chazal's statement on a verse in *Yechezkel* (34, 31): *"Atem keruim adam, v'ein umos ha'olam keruim adam"*; only Klal Yisrael are called *adam*, a person, whereas the nations of the world are not designated as such.

During the nefarious anti-Semitic Beilis trial in Russia, in 1913, a delegation of leading Jewish leaders was summoned to explain to the Russian courts many disparaging comments about non-Jews found in the pages of the Talmud. In response to the citation above, Rav Shapiro explained that *adam* is in the singular configuration. The Jewish People are called *adam* in the singular because we are of *one soul* and *one essence*. Unlike other nationalities, where if a member of their nation elsewhere suffers, it doesn't affect anyone beyond the individual themselves, Jews everywhere in the world hurt along with the sufferer. Similarly, if a Jew in a distant place commits a shameful crime, Jews everywhere are embarrassed by that wrongdoing, and indeed, non-Jews everywhere hold *all* B'nei Yisrael in contempt for that very reason. Conversely, when someone of the Jewish faith distinguishes themselves in a noteworthy way, Jews everywhere feel a deep sense of personal pride. This singular identification is because we are *adam*, one person.

My husband continued to cite the comment of our Sages, who explained how it was that the heathens were able to bring idolatrous symbols into the Holy of Holies of the Beis Hamikdash. They observed that it was only after Jews at the time had invited idolatry into their hearts and homes that Israel's enemies gained access to the heart of Hashem's home. Similarly, he argued, if we bring noxious cultural and societal influences into our lives, we become vulnerable to the dark forces that wait to discharge their venom upon us. Hence, my husband insisted, the only legitimate response to those who hate us is to strengthen ourselves from within by amplifying our personal and familial *kedushah*. He quoted the verse: "*V'ra'u kol amei ha'aretz, ki sheim Hashem nikra alecha, v'yaru mimeka*—And all the nations of the land will see that the name of G-d is upon you, and they will stand in fear of you" (*Devarim* 28:10). This commitment to growing in our spiritual discipline, he suggested, requires greater sensitivity in our interpersonal conduct, especially within the family, and greater caution in our use of contemporary technology.

As an aside, my sister, Rebbetzin Teitelbaum, related to me on the occasion of my father's yahrzeit that my father used to bemoan the advent of the telephone, which we hardly think of as being something that belongs in the category of a technological tool. My father used to say that prior to the proliferation of telephones, if one wanted to check on their parents or connect with friends, they would have to take the trouble, time, and effort to go to their home and see them face to face. Now, he lamented, as the saying goes, "Let your fingers do the walking." What a loss that is, he concluded, especially for elderly parents, who wait so eagerly for a visit from their children.

In my personal reflections on the various communal responses to the Pittsburgh tragedy, the Chanukah Monsey attack, and other recent tragedies, I noted that many voices called on Jewish institutions to increase their security measures, and likewise demanded that local police forces provide our synagogues and Jewish Centers with more protection. While there certainly is practical wisdom in that direction, we must not be misled into placing our faith in the wrong places. I was reminded of a Talmudic metaphor of a ship at sea that was desperate to find a safe place at which to disembark. At long last, they spotted what appeared to be a small island in the midst of the turbulent waters. Delighted, they made their way off the ship and set up housekeeping on the island. All went well until they decided to build a fire to provide them with warmth and the wherewithal to cook. No sooner was the fire lit than suddenly their "island" turned over, throwing them into the sea. What they had thought of as a benevolent space, a protective island hosting them, was in fact a large whale that became uncomfortable with the fire of its "settlers." Throughout our blood-drenched history, there have been many oases, many countries, that started out as inviting and hospitable. With time, however, they "turned" on us, and plotted our destruction. America has, thankfully, been a wonderful safe haven for Jews, but placing excess trust in anyone but Hashem, is ultimately misguided.

My husband concluded the event with the words of Yechezkel HaNavi (*Yechezkel* 34:27–31): "Then they will know that I am Hashem, when I break the rods of their yoke, and rescue them from the hand of those who enslave them. They will no longer be spoils for the nations, and the beast of the land will no longer devour them; they will dwell securely, and none will make them afraid…Now you are My sheep, the sheep of My pasture, *you* are **Man**; I am your G-d—this is the word of Hashem."

May it happen speedily in our days!

Chapter 32

The Self

Recently, I heard an interview with a secular author, who reported the results of research being done on a specific drug that promises to provide relief to people suffering from a variety of difficult-to-treat disorders, including depression, addiction, and anxiety, among others. In the process, the author discovered that these "remarkable substances" were capable of improving not only the lives of the mentally ill, but also of healthy people coming to grips with the challenges of everyday life. Until now, these drugs had been abused by people seeking "highs" and frequently ended with toxic consequences. However, in a controlled and guided environment and with the oversight of responsible physicians, trials were now being done in medical centers such as UCLA, NYU, and Johns Hopkins. One of the central issues under scrutiny is whether mental illness is biologically determined, i.e., the result of a chemical imbalance, or represents a loss of meaning in one's life. This research seeks, as one practitioner stated, to "wed the two approaches." The author speaks authoritatively because he personally subjected himself to one of the experimental trials. He describes the experience as one of "self-transcendence." He puts it this way: "We are born into an *egoless* world, but we live and die imprisoned within ourselves." He further describes what he encountered as an almost mystical experience where "the voice of the ego is muted or silenced." The message for him was that "so much human suffering stems from a preoccupation with 'self'; that humanity is trapped in a story that sees people as lonely, isolated agents acting in the world."

The author concludes that in this altered state of consciousness where his ego became dissolved, it became abundantly clear that life was about *relationships*; that we are all one, connected to the same source. That realization alone, he argued, can make our existence meaningful.

I always find it fascinating that as science expands its limited horizons, it comes closer and closer to what the Torah has taught all along. The persistent power of ego and the inability or resistance to recognizing our connectedness has, on a daily basis, compromised our well-being. Indeed, our Sages teach that the Torah wasn't given at Har Sinai until the Jewish People overcame their separateness and spoke as "one person with one heart." Unquestionably, it is the ubiquitous illusion of separateness that gives rise to our demonizing others and finding fault with them. It is noteworthy that the great Rabbi Akiva asserted, "*V'ahavta l'rei'acha kamocha zeh klal gadol baTorah*—And you should love your friend as yourself; this precept is a major principle of the Torah."

Rabbi Akiva underscores the importance of our oneness as a cardinal ideal toward which we should strive. In this regard, the Baal Shem Tov taught that when we see a shortcoming in others, it is a sign from Heaven that we should examine ourselves for that very fault. Invariably, he asserted, the deficiency is ours, and what we discern in others is a mirror image of ourselves.

"Separateness" is no small matter and exacts a great toll on mankind. The perception of separateness, the illusion that ego effectuates in our lives, is most evident in its impact on relationships.

What follows are situations where the effects of ego were prominent factors in determining the quality of the relationship:

- Suri and Yossi came in for counseling. Both are wonderful young people who cannot resolve or accept their differences. Yossi is a perfectionist who cannot abide a messy house, a lack of punctuality in picking up the kids from school, being late for appointments, or having meals thrown together at the last minute. He gets rattled by disarray of any kind. To compensate, Yossi takes over, steps into Suri's domain, pushes her aside, and insists on doing things his own way. Consistent with his perfectionism, Yossi is not a social butterfly and prefers his own company. Suri, while laid-back and admittedly not always on top of her "*balabusta* game," is a loving, considerate, and charming young woman. She is a great mom, and is very popular among her many friends. Both Yossi and Suri are locked in a battle of seeming incompatibility. Their bruised egos prevent them from accepting their separate realities and modus operandi. In this state of mind, they cannot see that their differences might potentially counterbalance what the other cannot bring to the relationship. Setting aside their egos would allow them to celebrate their differences as distinctions that can enhance their life together and that of their family.

- In contrast to this scenario is that of Naomi and Feivel, who demonstrated a refreshing approach to their new union, a second marriage for both of them. Naomi, with her ever-present smiling demeanor, responded to my question of how they were doing by giving me an insight into their respective personalities. She described herself as affectionate, demonstrative, and open, with constant words of praise. Feivel, on the other hand, was more reserved and not given to much verbal or effusive expressions of emotion. Naomi chose not to take his affect personally. She decided to set her ego aside and focus on Feivel's steadfastness and his remarkably disciplined approach to his daily routine, his Torah learning, his regular attendance to *minyanim*, and his timeliness at work. Though not as emotionally forthcoming as her deceased first husband, Naomi is determined to concentrate on his nature as a positive counterbalance to her own. Naomi's wise approach stems from the ability to set oneself aside, to park one's ego and embrace differences.

The case studies cited above are mere examples that, with slight variations, might very well be descriptions of our own lives. We, too, often stand on ceremony, insisting that life and the people in our lives must conform to our story. We dig in our heels and buy into the delusion of separateness, creating unnecessary barriers between ourselves and others.

To paraphrase a well-known statement, "One small step by man is a great step for mankind." That phrase rings true for all of us. *We* have to be the change that we want to see. In any encounter where we can invoke the "this is not about me" statement—where we can remove ourselves from the picture and see others as our sisters and brothers—we will have taken a huge step forward for mankind, bringing about the world Hashem promised us would be forthcoming, a world where we can appreciate that we are all of one piece in the service of the one G-d.

May that day come speedily in our time.

Chapter 33

Family First

I
t was with deep sadness that we received the news of the passing of Rabbi Ronnie Greenwald. Though we live a considerable distance from his center of activity, Rabbi Greenwald's influence and inspiration was felt everywhere, and no one will contest that our generation is orphaned by his loss. Rabbi Greenwald's involvement in a web of Jewish communal interests and concerns was far-reaching. As everyone who consulted him knew, there was nothing so great as to intimidate him, and nothing so small that he deemed it unworthy of his involvement. By all accounts, he was a living legend.

Like so many others, I turned to Rabbi Greenwald for his wise counsel when people asked me for help with their at-risk teens. No matter how many times I called, he was always forthcoming and eager to help however he could. What impressed me most, however, was his exhortation to people who, like he himself, work for the *klal* to be ever mindful of their foremost priority—their own families. He told me that he had encountered too many *kiruv* professionals whose families fell between the cracks. It's no secret in the world of *avodas ha'kodesh* that the risk of neglecting one's own family is a serious occupational hazard.

To be sure, it isn't for want of caring for our own. Rather, it's the perception of an urgent need "out there" that cannot wait—a perception all the more compelling and dangerous because it is true. The problem with surrendering to this urgency is that every "crisis" is quickly followed by another, while our children's formative years pass with too little input on our part (not to speak of the toll *klal* work exacts on the quality of spousal relationships). Attending to the needs of our family does not bring accolades and testimonials. It is sometimes more enjoyable to hang out with our friends. It is much easier to become heroes to those "out there." Moreover, those closest to us know our vulnerabilities and can push our buttons, evoking responses that are not always of the most exalted variety. This can move people to seek appreciation not forthcoming in their own homes, and, rather than face the issues, take the easy way out. Hence, many seek refuge in focusing outward rather than inward.

The voice of *mussar* in our generation, Rav Shlomo Wolbe, commented on a statement by renowned kabbalist Rav Chaim Vital asserting that a person's *middos* are measured first and foremost by how he relates to his wife and family. Rav Wolbe states that if a person does kindness like *tzedakah, bikur cholim, nichum aveilim,* and *simchas chassan v'kallah,* surely he will rejoice in Olam Haba. However, if an examination of the individual's relationship with his wife and family finds the opposite, it will cancel out all the good he has done for others. Rav Wolbe concludes with the plea that we exercise great caution to make sure that our good hearts are not directed outside, while negativity and mean-spiritedness reign within.

Since such gravity is attached to this concept in the Heavenly Court, it is to be expected that we find this principle of "family first" reflected in our halachic code. In delineating priorities in *tzedakah,* the *Shulchan Aruch* specifies that immediate family members come first, then relatives a bit further removed, followed by members of the local community, and finally, the poor of Eretz Yisrael. I am a big believer in the importance of friends and community, but the well-known adage that charity begins at home is an honored Jewish ideal.

A young friend of mine, Tanya, is a member of the "sandwich generation," meaning that she has both elderly parents and a household of children, married and single, who require her care and attention. She is often conflicted over who should take priority. On one occasion, Tanya's daughter traveled from overseas to have her first baby in the supportive company of her mother. At the same time, her mother suddenly took ill in a city at a considerable distance from Tanya's home. Tanya's father called in a panic, insisting that they needed her support at this critical juncture. Torn by this no-win situation, Tanya sought out an objective *posek* to determine her obligation. He ruled that in this particular instance, her mother came first.

Tanya commented that she was extremely grateful to be able to address this heart-wrenching quandary to a Torah authority. It relieved her of the guilt that would certainly have plagued her if she would have been forced to make this decision on her own. Taking counsel helps us verify the legitimacy of the demands made by family members. Care must be taken not to run ourselves ragged trying to respond to what others consider needs.

In contrast, a relative of one of our neighbors, Eli, related a similar dilemma. Eli is an only child who had just gotten off a coast-to-coast flight from visiting with his elderly father. No sooner had he walked through the door of his home than he got a call from his father, insisting that he return immediately. Distressed, Eli asked his father's caregiver if anything was amiss. Everything was in order, the aide said, but his father missed him. Gripped by guilt, Eli called his *rav*, who told him that while it would unquestionably be ideal to live closer to his father, he was under no obligation to fly back. Eli, like Tanya, was relieved to have the direction and support of a *psak*.

These are sensitive questions. Given the delicate nature of the variables, we would all be well-advised not to make decisions of this sort on our own. It behooves us to constantly reassess the fragile balance between attention to family and attention to friends and community. Both the wise words of Rabbi Ronnie Greenwald and the cautionary remarks of Rav Wolbe remind us that no less than eternity lies in the balance.

Chapter 34

Twins

L ife is a great teacher or, at the very least, a great initiator of curiosity. You may be pleased to learn that a number of recent events provoked my interest in the subject of twins. I discovered that the twin relationship provides a fascinating study in human nature. While most of my experience with twins is anecdotal, I do have some impressive credentials that qualify me as an authority in the field: My husband is a twin, and among our grandchildren, we have six sets of twins.

Counterintuitive as it may be, twins, despite their closeness, are more often than not opposites in temperament. That was true of my husband and his twin, who from their earliest years were almost diametrically opposed in nature. The same is also evident in the family of our son Rabbi Yakov Moshe. Rabbi Yakov and his family came recently for a visit. Among their delightful children are five-year-old twins, Chevy and Shevy (how's that for confusion?). Chevy is an easygoing, happy-go-lucky, absentminded charmer. Shevy, on the other hand, is a great student, quite intense, and an unrelenting perfectionist. An example of Shevy's perfectionism surfaced when she adamantly refused to go to sleep at night in a bed that we, in a frenzy to get going in the morning, had failed to make up. To Shevy, an unmade bed was anathema to her personality. Conversely, Chevy never took notice, and if she did, could care less. I had to chuckle. I found it so amusing that these two little beings who had together shared space in the same womb for nine months could emerge with such totally opposite dispositions.

Despite their dissimilar makeup, however, twins share a bond that goes far beyond the one that exists between single siblings. Psychologists in the field claim that there is proof that twins begin to communicate with each other as early as fourteen weeks in utero.

A couple of years ago, due to a mishap, my husband suffered a broken clavicle bone (collar bone). In excruciating pain on Shavuos night, he became very nauseous and began to vomit. In between heaves, he commented that it had been at least forty years since he last threw up. Realizing that he would not make it to shul the next morning, he lamented that it would be the first time in his adult life that he would miss the reading of the *Aseres Hadibros* and *Akdamos*.

On Motzaei Yom Tov, our children called from New York reporting that Uncle Aaron, my husband's twin brother, who lives in Brooklyn, had been sick, vomiting on Shavuos night, and had remarked to his wife that it had been more than forty years since he had last done so. Furthermore, he noted sadly, he had never in his life missed hearing the reading of the *Aseres Hadibros* and *Akdamos*.

We were all astonished. It was a combination of eerie and uncanny, and it spoke to a mysterious symbiotic connection that could neither be denied nor explained. Even beyond this particular episode, there were times over the years when my husband would pick up the phone in Milwaukee to call his brother in Boro Park because he had a sense that Aaron was not feeling well. Invariably he was right.

Indeed, our Sages (*Shemos Rabbah* 2:5) report the comment of Rabbi Yannai, who likens the relationship between Hashem and Israel to that of twins. He says, "Just as twins, when one feels pain in his head, so does his counterpart, so too with the Ribbono Shel Olam and His children, B'nei Yisrael, in the midst of their travail."

An inspiring event occurred some years back when my husband's twin, Rabbi (Professor) Aaron was being sworn in as Dean of Hofstra University's Law School. Apprised of the upcoming ceremony, my husband decided to surprise his brother by showing up for the occasion. My husband contacted the university program director, who was absolutely delighted with the idea. He picked us up with a limousine at the airport and happily acquiesced to my husband's request for five minutes during the induction ceremony to address the audience. Once again, the program director eagerly agreed. Upon our arrival, we were whisked away backstage in a hall filled with dignitaries, justices of the New York Supreme Court, many Law School professors, and a veritable who's who of the New York law scene. At the right moment in the program, the emcee announced that they had a surprise for Professor Twerski. When my husband came on stage, Rabbi Aaron did a double take, not believing his eyes. In my husband's brief remarks to a primarily secular audience, he quoted the Talmudic statement of our Sages that an angel is dispatched from Heaven to teach the infants the entirety of Torah—in utero—for the gestational duration of nine months. "As all of you may know," my husband continued, "Professor Twerski and I are twins, and we shared the same space for nine months, studying with an angel. I was born four minutes *before* my brother. Now, many of you know my brother, his type A personality, and his assertiveness; how would you explain his allowing me to emerge before him?

"Well, let me explain, Professor Twerski allowed me to go first because he knew that in so doing, he would have four minutes alone with the angel. I am telling you this information because I know enough about the responsibilities of a dean to know that eventually there will be complaints and criticisms that you will want to dump on him. Let me caution you, in advance, to remember before you do so that Professor Twerski is someone who had four minutes alone with an angel." The audience dissolved in appreciative laughter. It was a beautiful moment, attesting to the great love, not only of brothers to one another, but two brothers with the additional advantage of being twins.

To be sure, there are well-known challenges that have to be navigated with twins, such as competitiveness, parents giving each their due without bias, and celebrating each one's individuality. The advantages, however, are affirmed by studies that tell us that the greatest soothing that can be given to an agitated infant is to bring his twin into his proximity. As adults, and especially when there is a great geographic distance between them, it may not be so easy or immediate, but the symbiosis remains strong, inspiring, and heartwarming, nonetheless.

Wouldn't it be wonderful if we regarded everyone with even a little bit of that feeling of closeness?

PART VI

GRATITUDE

Chapter 35

Acknowledging the Good

One of the common side effects of getting older is a greater tendency to get sentimental. My friends and I—"older folks"—seem, somehow, to have a need for the familiar landscape in order to remain emotionally intact. Strangely, this need extends even to such things as insignificant as a local department store that has gone out of business. When one of the long-standing major department stores in Milwaukee declared recently that they were closing their doors, many of us senior citizens were upset. A landmark of scores of years was gone. It goes without saying that the loss of all too many dear friends in the last period of time has taken a huge emotional toll. Their indelible imprint is everywhere, and life is not the same without them. We appreciate what they gave us and the legacies they left us, but we miss them so much. Curiously, at the same time, the changes in our landscape have heightened our consciousness. We have a keener appreciation of our beloved families and dear friends, and a greater awareness of the blessings that surround us. *Hakaras ha'tov*, gratitude, has taken on new meaning, and has become a moment-to-moment feature of our existence. Previously, feeling and expressing gratitude was a more cerebral and deliberate experience that we knew had to be incorporated into our behaviors. Now, every move we make and every step we take brings us face to face with *hakaras ha'tov*. We take nothing for granted anymore.

Indeed, from a Torah perspective, gratitude, to be *"makir tov,"* is one of the major objectives and imperatives of creation. Mankind got off to a bad start when Adam HaRishon, confronted by Hashem after having eaten of the forbidden fruit, blamed his wife, Chavah, by telling Hashem, *"Ha'ishah asher nasata imadi*—The woman You gave me made me do it." The comment of our Sages is that Adam was a *"kafui tov,"* an ingrate. Instead of being thankful for the gift of Chavah, he shrugged off personal responsibility and thereby embedded into the DNA of humanity the challenge of cultivating the attribute of gratitude.

Rav Yitzchak Hutner, in his *sefer Pachad Yitzchak*, proposes that *hakaras ha'tov*, saying thank you, is one of the primary ways in which humanity maintains its dignity. Inasmuch as we are always on the receiving end, and are constantly the beneficiaries of Divine kindness, there is a deep and inescapable feeling of *bushah*, existential embarrassment. The only way for us to avoid these feelings is by giving Hashem in return our deepest appreciation, our *hakaras ha'tov*. Indeed, according to the *sefarim ha'kedoshim*, one of the objectives of B'nei Yisrael throughout history is to correct the catastrophic flaw of *kafui tov*, of being ingrates.

Reflect on the following: Our Sages teach that Moshe Rabbeinu's given name was "Tuvia," but that in recognition of Basya, Pharaoh's daughter, who saved his life and named him Moshe, meaning, "I drew him out of the water," Hashem Himself deferred to Basya and called him Moshe. Appreciation and gratitude trumped everything, even the preference of Moshe's parents.

A glance at the siddur and the *Shacharis* prayer amplifies the extent to which we are called upon to be conscious of and grateful for the many commonplace blessings we have. The morning benedictions range from an appreciation for being Jewish and free, to gratitude for the clothes we wear, to the ability to see, sit, stand, and walk. In the Shabbos liturgy, we have the *tefillah* of *Nishmas*, where we exclaim, "Even if our mouths were full of song like the ocean, and our tongues full of melody like the multitude of its waves, still we would fall short of being able to thank You for all Your kindnesses." Given the centrality of this value, it should not come as a surprise to us that the Torah's sensitivity to *hakaras ha'tov* extends even to inanimate objects. Our Sages emphasize that Moshe Rabbeinu was restricted from striking the Nile for the first two plagues against Egypt, and from striking the ground to bring about the third plague, lice, inasmuch as the Nile and the earth were helpful to him during his life. In the first instance, the river protected his wicker basket when Moshe's mother placed him as an infant in the reeds of the Nile, and in the second instance, the earth covered the body of the Egyptian taskmaster that Moshe killed.

Our son Rabbi Benzion shared that he remembers accompanying his father as a young child to a car dealer to trade in his jalopy for a more reasonable car. As they took leave, Rabbi Benzion said that my husband walked over to the car he was leaving behind and paused momentarily, lost in thought. When he questioned his father about what he was thinking, my husband responded that the car had given him many years of service and while one can't talk to an inanimate object, he felt that, at the very least, he could *feel* gratitude. It clearly left a huge impression, such that this many years later, the message still informs our son's life.

Conversely, our sacred texts make it clear that if one does not cultivate a sense of gratitude to one's fellow man, he will ultimately come to the point where he will defy even his Creator. A perfect example is the Pharaoh of Egypt who began his downward spiral with, "A new king who did not remember Yosef," i.e., the good that Yosef had done for his country. Predictably, this eventually led to Pharaoh's blasphemous question: "Who is G-d that I should listen to Him?" Such is the nature of this trajectory—first, one fails to recognize man; ultimately, he fails to recognize G-d.

Above all, we must remember that B'nei Yisrael are called *Yehudim*, the root word of which is *hodaah*, meaning "thanks" and "acknowledgment of good." We begin every day with **Modeh Ani**, from the same root word, thanking Hashem for life and the gift of another day.

Chapter 36

A Hand to Hold

T he precarious nature of life needs no explanation. The *sefarim* point out that our existence in this world is like a *galgal ha'chozer*, a turning wheel. One moment we might find ourselves on top of the heap, with good fortune smiling upon us, and the next moment the wheel turns and what we took for granted is gone. We are then confronted with a new reality and an unanticipated set of challenges.

Many who have sought our counsel have shared the difficult adjustments they had to make when their *parnasah* took an unfortunate dip. Too often *shalom bayis* is affected, and self-esteem—especially the husband's—is shattered. Such challenges test the couple's resilience as well as that of everyone in their sphere of influence.

As the wheel turns, life presents us with times of joy and times of loss. There is a well-known maxim that pain is inevitable but suffering is optional; when a family is in pain, their suffering can be mitigated by a supportive network of people who care, reach out with empathy, and let them know that they are not alone.

In a poignant piece entitled "Holding Hands," a writer tells the story of two children who were playing together on the beach, building an elaborate sandcastle. They laughed gleefully as their creation grew to an impressive size, evoking admiring comments from passersby. Suddenly, a big wave came along and knocked the castle down, reducing it to a heap of wet sand. The author writes, "Remarkably, instead of bursting into tears over their ruined project, the two children ran to another spot on the shore, laughing and holding hands, and sat down to build another castle."

The author concludes that he learned an important lesson. "All things in our lives, all the complicated structures we spend so much time and energy creating, are built on sand. Only our relationships to other people endure. Sooner or later, a wave will come along and knock down what we have worked so hard to build up. When that happens, only the individual who has somebody's hand to hold will be able to laugh."

Holding hands takes many forms. Gratitude is one of them. It is one of the most powerful ways to let others know that what they have worked so hard to build will not be washed away and forgotten.

I will never forget Chaikie, a distant cousin of my husband who lived in London and came to Milwaukee for a visit when I was still a young newlywed. She walked into my kitchen, tall, reserved, and of regal bearing, and out of the clear blue she disintegrated into a pool of tears. Between sobs she told me her story.

She had been married for over twenty years to a wonderful man named Mendel. Several months ago, he had died very suddenly; he had been relatively young, with no significant health issues. Chaikie stated brokenheartedly that she could come to terms with her devastating loss, except for one thing that gave her no peace. She had never taken the time to tell Mendel how much he meant to her. She had figured that there was no urgency…there was always tomorrow.

Chaikie learned the hard way that tomorrow is not guaranteed. Before she left, she appealed to me, no matter how busy and demanding life became, never to put off telling the people I love and cherish how much they mean to me.

I hereby pass her important message to you.

Chapter 37
Reciprocal Relationship

There is so much to be thankful for:

- When Chantzi called and asked to meet with me at the earliest opportunity, I sensed excitement in her voice. Intrigued, I arranged to see her at once. She arrived with a beaming face, a smile that went from ear to ear, and confided that after many failed attempts, she was finally expecting a child. Thrilled and grateful, Chantzi wanted to know how she might show her gratitude to Hashem for His great kindness and love.

- Merrick, a long-time aspirant to *frumkeit*, had over the years made great strides in integrating Yiddishkeit into his life. The crowning achievement for him, however, was when he successfully married off all his children to Jewish spouses. Grateful and humbled by his good fortune, he wanted to express gratitude to Hashem in a tangible way. In that moment, he made a decision to move from the affluent neighborhood where he lived to a more modest but Jewishly stronger neighborhood where he would be able to become fully *shomer Shabbos*. He felt that G-d had reached

132

out to him and it was obligatory upon him to acknowledge that Divine attention with something in return.

- Fishel, after a long, frustrating period of seeking husbands for his daughters, finally hit the jackpot. Teary-eyed at the milestone that had so long eluded him, he approached his rabbi with an offer to defray the wedding expenses of one of the *kehillah's balebatim* who was less able to meet the steep cost of a wedding for his child. He felt that he wanted to give back, to show *hakaras ha'tov* to his benevolent Heavenly Father.

The common denominator in these cases is the intent not only to feel grateful, but to actualize that feeling in a palpable act, expressing thanks for the Ribbono Shel Olam's intervention in one's life.

Gratitude and its expression are powerful factors in moving people to achievements that they might not have reached without them. A well-known chapter in the Torah captures this principle dramatically: We know that Yaakov Avinu favored his son Yosef with a *kesones pasim*, a coat of many colors, a distinction which brings upon Yosef the jealousy of his older brothers. Indeed, the Gemara warns: "A person should never show favor to one child above the next, because due to Yaakov Avinu presenting Yosef with a garment worth not more than two *sela'im*, his brothers were jealous, which in turn led to the events that brought our ancestors down to Mitzrayim" (*Shabbos* 10b). Since the protagonist in this narrative was none other than Yaakov, we must assume he understood the risks of his actions. What compelling reason would persuade him to set aside this obvious concern?

While the commentaries suggest many possible reasons, a recent *shiur* from our son Reb Efraim of Chicago, which addressed this very issue, resonated with me. He cited *Rashi's* comment that notes striking parallels between the painful events of Yaakov's life and that of Yosef. Yaakov judged that Yosef, like himself, was destined to spend many years in a morally corrosive environment, and thus would need something "extra" to preserve his integrity. Hence, he presented his son with a token of love, a special indication of how precious Yosef was to him, which would fortify him in the years ahead.

That this strategy worked is evidenced by a comment of our Sages: When Yosef was on the verge of succumbing to the seduction of Potifar's wife, it was the image of his saintly and loving father that saved him.

There is an important message in the Yaakov/Yosef drama for us, as we parent the future generations of Klal Yisrael. We must never forget how potent a force love is in building the character and moral resilience of our children. Children who feel loved and respected by parents are loath to trade that in, and are much less likely to disappoint that love by betraying the values of those who consider them so precious.

Reb Efraim took this conclusion a step further, suggesting that the same dynamic should apply to our relationship with our Father in Heaven. Recognizing and acknowledging Hashem's presence in our lives should make us want to respond gratefully, with fidelity to His Torah.

May we have the presence of mind to emulate the Chantzis, Merricks, and Fishels in acknowledging the loving embrace of *Hashem Yisbarach*, our Heavenly Father, moment to moment in our lives. And may we, as they did, find ever greater ways of serving Him with our love.

PART VII

WORDS AND ACTION

Chapter 38

Change:
It's Never Easy

One Shabbos some time ago, my six-year-old great-grandson, Sruli, waved to me from across the street where he lives, motioning that he would like to walk to shul with me. A warm, delightful, and gregarious child, he, like most youngsters his age, proceeded to carry on a conversation that resembled a stream of consciousness. Not yet jaded by life, Sruli commented on pretty much everything he saw along the way, which in this case consisted of the striking autumn foliage. The fall season had already begun its sweep of Wisconsin, and the streets were strewn with a gazillion multicolored leaves of various shapes, sizes, and textures. Sruli drew my attention to their beautiful hues of red, orange, brown, and yellow, and even on occasion, some remnants of their former green. "Bubby," he asked, "why are the fallen leaves and those about to fall so much more colorful than the ones still attached to the branches?"

I tried, with only moderate success, to distill my quasi-scientific knowledge of horticulture to a six-year-old's level. Simultaneously, I wondered how I might explain to him that this phenomenon provides a powerful lesson on the human existential struggle. In life, we are often "as a driven leaf," free to move in any direction and drawn to immerse ourselves in things that present themselves with enchanting, beguiling, captivating, and seductive colors. The caveat, however, is that the duration of these fallen leaves is short. They shrivel up, dry out, and lose their beautiful colors in short order. Their counterparts, the less exciting green leaves that are still firmly attached to the branches, although not as enticing, are more tenacious and durable.

Our precious Torah is referred to as *Eitz Chaim*—the "Tree of Life." As long as we are connected and attached to its branches, we are alive. If, Heaven forbid, we allow ourselves to be severed from our Source, though things may seem "colorful" at first, it signals the beginning of our demise.

I am reminded of Judy, a highly intelligent and spiritual individual who came into our orbit many years ago. Judy was a very ardent young woman and took on the practice of Judaism with an unhealthy intensity. My mother, in situations such as this, would comment that "*Mehn tzeet ibur dos strickel*," the Yiddish aphorism suggesting that one is "pulling the string too tightly." Judy would beat herself up at the slightest perceived infraction and was mercilessly self-critical. Predictably, she crashed. She threw off the practice of Torah and mitzvos, electing for herself instead the life of the "driven leaf"—a seductive existence of "freedom" and permissiveness. When she visited us sometime later, she described to us how she was drinking from every stream of pleasure. Judy applied the same intensity that had characterized her previous behavior to her new lifestyle. Not surprisingly, the colors of her "driven leaf" mode soon began to fade. The last time I saw her was at a chance meeting at the airport. The initial sheen, effervescence, and excitement of her latest experiment were gone. Judy looked spent, tired, and old beyond her years.

The ebb and flow of the changing seasons of life beg the question of whether we have incorporated the changes we envisioned into our current lives, or whether we have settled back into the status quo and continued on with business as usual.

No one will challenge the fact that change is difficult. The distractions—family responsibilities and the need to earn a living, to name two of the more prominent preoccupations—are enemies of growth. Most often, our defense is that we really do want to live up to our potential but that we are waiting for a better time, the most opportune moment, to make changes. The reality is that only a conscious and deliberate move to give expression to goals *through action* will overcome our inertia. Dreams and aspirations alone will get us nowhere.

Dr. Jonice Webb, a well-known psychologist and author, warns against three pitfalls:

- **Expecting growth to be linear**. Drawing upon the metaphor of a ladder, it is to be expected that we will sometimes take two steps up and one step down. The key is to keep working persistently until we make progress toward our goal.
- **Responding negatively to failure**. The danger of feeling like a failure when suffering a setback is that this can turn into self-anger, a major deterrent to progress. Self-contempt can easily send us off-track or set us back.
- **Giving up**. People commonly believe that if you momentarily lose your way, you might as well give up. But losing your way temporarily is absolutely okay and is immaterial to your ultimate success, as long as you don't give up.

Clearly, everyone has to choose for himself a particular area of challenge in which to grow. For me, a definitive marching order is implicit in *Sefer Bereishis*. Hashem brought the world into being by utterances, using words such as "Let there be light" and "Let there be vegetation." The world we occupy became real with words. We too, created as we are in Hashem's image, create *our* world with the words we utter. The nature and quality of that world—our relationships with our spouse, children, relatives, and friends—is in great measure dependent on our words. Are they positive, validating, supportive, and encouraging, or are they negative, hurtful, and damaging?

Let us assess our use of words with friends and family. Let us reconnect to the Tree of Life, the Torah, and let us keep growing!

Chapter 39

Footsteps

Shortly after Pesach, when our children from Yerushalayim were getting ready to leave, their one-year-old son, Yankela, took his first steps. We were all gathered in the kitchen at the time, and Yankela just stood up and toddled forward. We all shrieked in delight, calling for everyone nearby to come see this delightful milestone. It was a very special moment.

As the family celebrated, I recalled a conversation with my mother-in-law, *a"h*, many years ago. A *meshulach* had just left the house after being treated to his first decent meal in many days. My mother-in-law commented that all too often, *meshulachim* are not respectably received—partly because the hosts will have to part with some money, and partly because these visits are an intrusion on family time or other activities.

My mother-in-law recalled that a *meshulach* was present when one of her own children took his first steps, and everyone clapped and rejoiced. The *meshulach* watched the merriment and observed pensively, "I'm sure that when I took my first steps, there was also much celebration and happiness, but now, wherever I go, my footsteps are not received with much excitement."

A difficult but important insight. How do we greet others when we first see them? How do we make them feel?

Chapter 40
Words

Our youngest son-in-law, a long-time resident of Eretz Yisrael, keeps in touch with the country's breaking news, and learned recently that the producers of a certain brand of water and rice were claiming that their products were of superior quality to any such similar products on the market. The reason for their unique excellence, the manufacturers claimed, was because throughout the process of production, both the rice and the water were spoken to warmly, with complimentary words of encouragement, to give forth the best they had within them.

Needless to say, many scoffed at what sounded so ludicrous. The idea that positive words could affect inanimate objects such as rice and water seemed preposterous. Whether there is any validity to that claim is certainly questionable. However, without question, human beings, both children and adults, thrive and blossom on words of encouragement.

Eric Fromm, a major humanistic philosopher and psychoanalyst of the last century, in an essay entitled "The Art of Loving," wrote that basic nourishment is represented by milk, which is a newborn's first food. As a rule, the world's mothers provide the requisite nourishment for their growing children, the fundamental "milk" for their progress, until the children reach the age of independence. There are, however, those who go beyond basic sustenance and provide not only "milk," but "honey" and its sweetness, which represent emotional nurturing and affirmation. Fromm's conclusion is that when we meet people, it becomes abundantly clear to us who was raised with "milk" alone, and who was raised with "milk and honey." The confidence and self-esteem of the latter far surpass that evidenced by the former.

Fromm's essay came to mind when I met with Rachel, a stunningly beautiful young woman, who was expecting her first child. Rachel, a conflicted soul, came to see me in the throes of trying to sort out the impending decisions she would soon have to make. She related that she grew up with an emotionally compromised mother who targeted her with many angry outbursts and unending criticisms. It came to the point where, as a youngster, Rachel was convinced that *she* was responsible for her mother's psychological dysfunction. She recalled sadly that in her mother's eyes, she could never do anything right. Rachel's problem now was that when her mother found out that she was having a baby, she informed Rachel that she was flying out to help her. While Rachel could use the help, she was reluctant to open up the wounds of the past. Rachel shuddered at the thought of having to contend with the person who not only deprived her of "honey" in her formative years but gave her "milk" that was sour and rancid.

A similar case, but with a different outcome is Heshy. Heshy related how his father clipped his wings early in life with an incessant barrage of hurtful criticisms. His father's berating and injurious comments left their imprint such that Heshy grew up with trust issues and a devastatingly poor sense of self. As a result, Heshy personally sabotaged every possibility of a *shidduch*. Additionally, in desperation to shore up the black hole in his psyche, Heshy sought out only those who would worship him. He needed, at all times, to be placed on a pedestal. Narcissism became his refuge and even the counsel of those who cared about him fell on deaf ears.

I have mentioned and written before that I credit my father, *a"h*, for my resilience and ability to deal with contentious people in my adult life. As a youngster, I would frequently overhear my father's conversations with his friends where he would proudly boast about my achievements.

The experience of knowing how highly my father thought of me warmed me and invested me with a strength that I have been able to draw on in the dark nights that are invariably a part of life.

I also credit Mr. Naffetone, my English teacher of some sixty years ago, with playing a role in launching my writing "career." After reading one of my assigned pieces, he commented that he sees a book in my future. His statement, while quite simple and uncontrived, had the ability to engender a sense of confidence that would have far-reaching effects.

Emboldened by my experience, I have since advised spouses, parents, teachers, and friends of the power of complimenting their loved ones, not only to their face, but also allowing them to overhear the positive comments about them to others. The caveat, however, is that the praise must be sincere, and not fabricated. The effort made to catch our friends doing something right, while not always easy, can be a game changer in their lives. The power of making someone feel good about themselves cannot be overestimated. Sadly, the converse is also true. A steady diet of put-downs by an important figure in one's life can have a devastating effect that may require years of therapy to neutralize.

I suspect that most if not all of us, regret missed opportunities where we might have interacted more positively with others. To err is human, and unquestionably, we have all tried to do our best given the resources at our disposal at any given time. The good news is that hope springs eternal; though we cannot recapture lost moments, we can move forward in a positive direction, take ownership of past mistakes, and do our best to make amends before time runs out.

"*B'derech she'adam rotzeh leilech molichin oso.*" Paraphrased, this asserts that one is granted assistance from Heaven to navigate the path one chooses. We can choose the high road. May Hashem support our choice with success.

Chapter 41

Sharing

Rabbi Yaakov Weinberg, the late Rosh Yeshiva of Ner Israel in Baltimore, visited Milwaukee some forty-five years ago as a scholar-in-residence for our community. He taught in his inimitably brilliant and unequivocal manner, conjuring the image of a prophet expounding words of the Living G-d with fiery conviction.

In the audience was an academically accomplished young woman, who took great pride in her intellectual capacities and was predictably on guard. Impressed by the strength of Rabbi Weinberg's presentation, she raised her hand and inquired how one can achieve the level of certainty so manifest in his delivery.

Rabbi Weinberg perceived where she was coming from and what she was asking. "You need to know," he told her, "that counterintuitive as it may seem, it is only in giving yourself up that you find yourself." Certitude in faith, the rabbi was saying, like many other essentials in life, can only take place when we get *ourselves* out of the way and make room for it to enter.

As I grow older, I find this paradox to be one of the most fundamental precepts in life. Letting go of immersion in self and ego liberates us to connect first and foremost to the Ribbono Shel Olam, and with every-one and everything else.

A heartwarming occurrence recently demonstrated this point. We were hosting members of the local Bandos family for our Friday night *seudah*. The senior Bandoses, Reb Efraim Fishel and his wife, are Holocaust survivors and, both well into their nineties, are sharp as a tack. They met in Bergen-Belsen after the war, married, made their way to this country, and ultimately settled in Milwaukee, where they raised two daughters and a son and lived most of their married life. Recently, they celebrated their sixty-eighth wedding anniversary.

This past year they decided to make aliyah to Eretz Yisrael, where they have children and many grandchildren. This was to be their last week in Milwaukee. The discussion during the *seudah* drifted toward the shifting values in our society and the dearth of solid relationships. Unspoken was the desire to find out the secret of the wonderful and durable marriage of this venerable couple.

The answer emerged unexpectedly as my husband was about to deliver his *d'var Torah*, which everyone anticipated would address this obvious question. Quite abruptly, Mr. Bandos, an otherwise very retiring and soft-spoken person, raised his voice to inquire if his wife could change seats with a younger guest for the duration of the talk so that she might better hear the Rabbi's words. It was a request that demanded a bit of maneuvering and shifting of chairs, but reasonable enough, and every-one moved to make the necessary accommodations.

The request, as requests go, was modest indeed, but it represented the answer we were all looking for, the key component to a beautiful and lasting marriage. Mr. Bandos was looking out for his wife's best inter-est. His focus was not on himself, but on the pleasure of his spouse. In this very sweet, unassuming, and genuine way, he captured the essence of any relationship: the ability to climb out of one's self and focus on the other. At the end of the day, the beneficiary is the person who is able to do this. It is he who becomes a bigger and better individual.

At a *sheva berachos* a few years ago, I was privileged to hear some *divrei berachah* from Rabbi Dr. Jerry Lob, who recounted an insightful anec-dote about Rav Chaim Shmuelevitz, renowned *mashgiach* of the Mir

Yeshiva. On one occasion, he was walking with a group of *talmidim* when they passed a children's shoe store and noticed a young woman entering the store with a toddler in tow. The *mashgiach*, sensing a lesson to be learned, instructed his students to follow him inside. They watched as the child was fitted for his first pair of shoes and could not help but be impressed by the joy reflected in the radiance of the mother's face. Rav Chaim turned to his students and said, "I wanted you to experience this, because the ability to share in someone else's joy and happiness is something that even in Gan Eden cannot be observed or duplicated."

Similarly, it is a well-known fact that Rav Chaim's family would hide the newspaper from him, fearing that he would find out that yet another soldier's life had been taken, and be plunged into inconsolable grief. He would then invariably seek out the family of the deceased and pay a shivah call, cry with them, and do everything in his power to comfort and console. Afterward, he would tell his students that this, too, is something Gan Eden cannot provide.

The common denominator in both events—whether sharing in a mother's delight of her child's first pair of shoes or sitting with a bereaved family—is the concept of being *nosei b'ol im chaveiro*, sharing in the burdens and experiences of one's fellow man. This happens when one lets go of self and makes room for the rich spectrum of life to expand in one's heart and mind. When we manage to transcend ego, we create space to notice others and join them wholeheartedly in both their joys and their sorrows. Ultimately, this enriching experience is possible only in this world. In the World to Come, great as it might be, this will not be an option.

Mr. Bandos embraced this concept and with it built a beautiful marriage of sixty-eight years and, *im yirtzeh Hashem*, many more. Likewise, Rabbi Weinberg in his great wisdom pointed a young woman seeking truth and fulfillment in the same direction.

The extent to which we can let go of preoccupation with self will determine the extent to which we will be able to enlarge and broaden the horizons of our existence. The extent to which we can get past our own desires will determine the depth of our relationships with others.

Chapter 42

The Holy and the Mundane

Not long ago, I was invited to participate in a seminar in Los Angeles on the topic "Jewish Mothers." I deliberated before accepting because at the time I felt ill, tired, and weak. Nevertheless, I decided to go, mostly because my host was to be my dear friend, Devorah Friedman, the esteemed Rebbetzin of Rabbi Aharon Dov Friedman, a distinguished Torah scholar in the LA community. It turned out to be just what the doctor ordered. I was treated to homemade yogurt, organic fruits and vegetables, sourdough bread, soups, and delicacies all made from scratch in the Friedman kitchen by Devorah. My health began to improve immediately. It is amazing how food—and the love that goes into it—can build relationships.

In truth, culinary delights are only a small feature of the stellar Friedman household. The Friedman's home is a *kiruv* sanctuary for people from all walks of life, whose search for meaning bring them to the Friedman doorstep.

During my stay, Devorah and her talented daughter, Liba, made a beautiful brunch for a group of women, many of them *baalos teshuvah* who have been nurtured and guided by the Friedmans. It was clear that these women came to learn, be challenged, and to avail themselves of the Torah perspective on life issues. They were, for the most part, women who made courageous transitions without family support. Their eagerness to follow the Torah path, regardless of the cost, was heartwarming and inspirational to observe.

At the main event on the topic "Jewish Mothers," the featured speakers, in addition to myself, were women whose fathers were *Gedolei HaTorah*, and whose mothers were wives whose singular devotion and self-sacrifice enabled their husbands to achieve their greatness. The daughters of these inspired women reminisced about their mother's remarkable qualities and gave the seminar's attendees much to think about.

After the seminar, I returned to the Friedman home uplifted and moved, yet weary and spent. Within moments, Devorah's vibrant health cuisine had me back on my road to recovery.

It struck me then that, counterintuitive as it may be, food is not just food. There are so many memories associated with the foods our mothers and grandmothers made for us and hopefully, in the future, with the foods that we provide for our progeny, family, and guests.

My older children practically salivate when they speak of my mother's—their Bubby's—breakfast salad. My mother, *a"h*, hand-grated the cucumbers, tomatoes, and radishes such that the juice released tasted heavenly when bread was dipped into it. Additionally, her challah and potato kugel, all made by her tired, worn-out hands, knew no parallel.

My children also often recall their Sunday visits to their Milwaukee Bubby, my mother-in-law's home, where they were always treated to scrumptious salmon patties and spaghetti "with-or-without ketchup," and her signature sponge cake and *mandelbrodt*. In addition, my children will tell you that they knew that my parents, Bubby and Zeide, were coming to visit from New York because for weeks prior to their arrival, the house smelled of my father's favorite foods, stuffed cabbage and chopped herring.

About forty years ago, Milwaukee hosted a SEED program from the Ner Israel Yeshiva of Baltimore. For several successive years, young men

from the yeshiva would come and spend the summer in Milwaukee, offering their teaching services to members of our community. Invariably,
they would spend the intervening Shabbosos with us. Great memories
were fostered as they sat at our *tish*, devouring *divrei Torah*, *niggunim*,
and Shabbos delicacies. When we meet with these now mature, accomplished Torah scholars, many in their grandfatherly stage, they wax
nostalgic about those wonderful days and the fabulous experience it
had been for them. Interestingly, what rates *most* prominently in their
recollections are the delicious brownies and the pungent homemade
pickles that graced our table! The music and the *divrei Torah*, inspiring
as they were, were not the first thing that came to mind, and mind you,
so many years have passed in the interim. Nothing, it seems, can com-
pete with brownies and pickles!

Another anomaly, consistent with the above, surfaces when my
daughters, who are far better cooks than I am, come to visit. Invariably,
my neighbors—who are gifted chefs—will want to help me welcome
my guests by bringing various delights from their kitchen. I present my
children with challahs, cakes, and foods far superior to my own. Their
response is always, "No, Mom, we want only yours." Clearly, more than
anything else, it is the unique memories and associations that are the
chief ingredients.

If all this seems trivial, it is important to underscore that our *Torah
ha'kedoshah* does not marginalize the physical, including the tasty and
nutritious foods that sustain life. As we extol in the Shabbos *zemiros*,
"*Basar v'dagim v'chol mataamim*"—Shabbos is celebrated with "meat, fish
and many culinary delights." Additionally, every Yom Tov has its distinct
flavors; milchig on Shavuos, matzah on Pesach, apples and honey on
Rosh Hashanah, kreplach and stuffed cabbage on Sukkos and Simchas
Torah, latkes and donuts on Chanukah, and hamantaschen on Purim.

There is a beautiful story told of Rabbi Dovid'l Lelover, a great
Chassidic luminary. On one of his travels, he passed through a village
where one of his childhood friends lived. He stopped in to visit with his
friend, whom he had not seen in many years. His friend, delighted and
deeply honored by the appearance of the great *tzaddik*, ran excitedly to
ask his wife to prepare some food worthy of so exalted a guest. His wife

responded that in their state of poverty, other than flour and water, she had no oil, eggs, yeast, salt, or sugar with which to prepare anything worthy of serving. Imploring her to do the best she could, he returned to entertain his esteemed guest while his wife mixed water to the flour and presented the Rebbe with a meager "flat-cake" offering.

Subsequently, in a letter to his wife, Reb Dovid'l reported that when he had visited with his childhood friend, he was served a delicacy that tasted like Gan Eden. The Lelover Rebbetzin, knowing that her husband was not given to notice—let alone comment on—food, dispatched a letter to the woman, asking for the recipe. The woman responded that since she had been working with nothing other than flour and water, she had turned her eyes heavenward and said, "Please, Hashem, we have such a distinguished guest and all I have to offer is this little bit of flour and water. I importune You, dear G-d, please put into my dough the spice of Gan Eden to give it flavor." She concluded, "Evidently, your husband being such a great *tzaddik*, he tasted my *tefillah*, the taste of Gan Eden that Hashem put in."

Gan Eden can be experienced in many ways. Unquestionably, learning Torah and doing mitzvos is the most straightforward approach. However, implausible as it may seem, we dare not minimize the ability to introduce Gan Eden into our servings through the *kavanos*, the thoughts and feelings, we have when we prepare the food for our families.

The taste of Gan Eden is still accessible.

Chapter 43
Life

I n a rare moment of solitude, my eyes drifted to a picture on the wall of my dining room. It was a picture of my father, *z"l*, taken on the occasion of my daughter Yocheved's *sheva berachos* some thirty-five years ago. Sitting at the table in this picture were my father, our son-in-law's grandfather, the *Minchas Yitzchak* (the Yerushalayimer Rav), and my husband. In addition, the picture shows some of my nephews, then young children, standing on all sides, listening raptly as my father was holding forth. The energy, the joy, and the humor are palpable from the expressions on everyone's faces. In the background, one can see my china cabinet, the very same china cabinet that adorns my dining room to this day. Nostalgic and almost weepy, I was gripped by how absurd and senseless it seemed that an inanimate piece of wood, the cabinet, is still extant, unaffected by time, while my father—the beloved and vibrant personality who transformed every occasion into a happening—has passed on, reduced to a two-dimensional picture on the wall.

From there, my mind went to an essay by Rav Chaim Shmuelevitz, the famous Mirrer Mashgiach, on the meaning of life. Rav Chaim addresses the puzzling statement of our Sages, who identify four categories of people who, while strictly speaking are physically alive, are nonetheless considered "dead." These are:

- A poor person
- One who has no children
- A blind person
- One afflicted with *tzaraas* (a form of leprosy)

Rav Shmuelevitz's essay clarified for me what otherwise appears to be a very harsh comment by Chazal. Rav Shmuelevitz addresses a common thread linking these categories of people, which potentially renders them lifeless. He posits that what qualifies someone to merit the title of life is the wherewithal to be a *giving* being. Created, as man is, in G-d's image, it behooves man to emulate Hashem in the quality of being the quintessential Giver. When one is denied or forfeits the capacity to *give*, to see beyond themselves, they might be existing in a physical sense, but bereft of the Divine image, they are not really "alive" in the truest sense of the word.

A poor person, whose poverty limits his ability to give to others, or a blind person who, similarly, cannot see others, is considered lifeless. Likewise, a childless person, who has no one to focus on beyond himself, and a leper, who, in the times of the Beis Hamikdash, was isolated from other people. The *metzora* was banished to the outskirts of the city, where he was quarantined in a state of *badad*, total isolation. He was not even allowed to interact with others similarly relegated to se-clusion. Obviously, this rendered him off limits, with no opportunity to *give* to others.

Rav Shmuelevitz goes on to emphasize that these categories are met-aphors that drive home the message that *giving* is the essence of life.

We all know people who transcend their circumstances and serve as inspiring models of giving, contributing significantly to society.

In the secular world, Hellen Keller, who became deaf and blind due to an illness in early childhood, demonstrated that even the most for-midable handicaps cannot obstruct a person from making meaningful contributions to society. We all know people who are not blessed with children yet give of themselves selflessly and generously to others and are integral and beloved members of their families, quintessential givers in every sense of the word. Many who are "poor" in monetary resources, choose nonetheless, to give of themselves—their time, effort, and energy—to enrich the lives of others.

The Biblical leper, a condition extinct in our time, was afflicted because of his antisocial attributes and conduct, with a disease that halachically removed him from society. The objective was to force him to recognize and repair his shortcomings. Metaphorically, individuals who are ill or suffer significant pain are frequently seen turning inward, focusing exclusively on themselves and their pain. In doing so, they progressively remove themselves from friends and family. In this category, as well, one can choose to focus either on the proverbial bars that imprison them or look through those bars to connect and make a difference.

It was Moshe Rabbeinu who identified the end of his life as the time when he could no longer teach and mentor. He realized that his journey as the faithful redeemer and shepherd of Israel had come to a close when his capacity to *give* was compromised.

My eyes wandered back to the picture of my father, and the china closet in the background. The china closet is—indeed, as it was then—silent, unchanged, and irrelevant. My father and the *Minchas Yitzchak*, on the other hand, are very much alive. Not only because their *neshamos* are immortal and live on in the *Olam Ha'emes*, but because they were givers. They gave abundantly during their lifetimes and continue to give and inspire even now. *"Tzaddikim b'misasam keru'im chayim*—The righteous even in death are considered alive." Indeed, they are still with us, escorting us and guiding us through the mountains and valleys of our existence.

What can we give to others? What can you give to others?

Chapter 44
Interacting with the World

Where visiting some dear friends when their doorbell rang. My friend Chani went to the door and returned with a big smile on her face. A young African-American boy, Marcus, had come to show her his report card.

Marcus was fourteen years old, Chani told us, and his single mother was ailing. Some months earlier, he had approached her to ask if there were any odd jobs he could do to make some money. Chani hired him to mow the lawn, rake the leaves, and clean the premises, which he did quickly and expertly.

He proved to be reliable, and for the next several months assisted her with chores. It was a win-win situation for everybody: Marcus felt empowered, and Chani had the work done. He loved coming around, and on this occasion, he had come to show her his report card. He told Chani he knew she would be proud.

I was touched by Chani's sensitivity to a child who had very little going for him, and for whom this act of kindness might serve to keep on the straight path. A significant *kiddush Hashem*, in a quiet and modest way.

Some years ago, Gary Torgow, a pillar of the Detroit Jewish community, was the guest speaker at a communal event. He related a moving anecdote about Neil Shine, the editor of the *Detroit Free Press*, a newspaper very favorable to Israel and the Jewish community.

His mother had immigrated to the United States years earlier in the month of December. She took a position as a housekeeper for a prominent Orthodox Jewish family who lived adjacent to the local synagogue. The family went on vacation in mid-December, promising to return on the twenty-fifth of the month.

Knowing nothing of Jewish practice, and since the family would apparently have no time to do it themselves, the well-intended new housekeeper took it upon herself to buy a large tree, decorate it, and bedeck the house with tinsel and festive lights. When the family returned, they found their house festooned with the gamut of holiday paraphernalia, their open living room window showcasing an adorned tree to the entire neighborhood.

At first, they thought they had arrived at the wrong block. After circling the block a few times to make sure that it was indeed their house, they made their way inside to find a beaming housekeeper. She proudly explained that she wanted to surprise them, knowing they wouldn't have time to prepare for the holiday. The *baal ha'bayis* acknowledged her thoughtful intentions, lauded her goodwill, and promised her a generous bonus—before he gently explained that Jews don't celebrate December 25th the way the non-Jewish world does.

Years later, at a dinner honoring that very *baal ha'bayis*, Mr. Shine was the featured speaker. He shared with the crowd that his affinity for both the Jewish People and the State of Israel was in great part a result of the respectful way this family had treated his mother, who had unwittingly caused them considerable embarrassment. A significant *kiddush Hashem*, with far-reaching consequences.

Some years ago, Professor Yaffa Eliach published a book entitled *Hassidic Tales of the Holocaust*. One of the people she interviewed was the the Bluzhever Rebbe, Rabbi Yisroel Spira, who recounted his survival of many harrowing, near-death situations. One sticks in my mind: As Rav of Bluzhev during the prewar years, on his way to shul every morning, he would warmly greet his non-Jewish neighbor with a hearty, "Good morning, Herr Schmidt!" to which Herr Schmidt would respond with an equally warm, "Good morning, Herr Rabbiner!"

When the war broke out, the Rebbe, with his townspeople, was sent together to the Janowska concentration camp. As he approached the officer waving people to life and death, he recognized the man as none other than his neighbor—Herr Schmidt.

"Good morning, Herr Schmidt," the Rebbe said, with the familiarity of old times.

Startled, Herr Schmidt looked up to see the emaciated figure of his old neighbor. "Good morning, Herr Rabbiner," he said. In deference to the man who had respectfully greeted him, he waved the Rebbe to the right—to life.

Yet another modest *kiddush Hashem* with far-reaching consequences.

While we must always be careful to conduct ourselves with integrity and sensitivity to our gentile hosts in *galus*, we must be cautious about judging the sometimes-harsh attitudes some Jews have toward the non-Jewish world. This is especially true of those who have suffered grievously at the hands of brutal anti-Semitic attacks. I still vividly remember my high school history teacher, who elaborated on the ongoing enmity of the non-Jewish world toward our people and urged the class to maintain a strong enmity to *goyim*. One classmate raised her hand and objected. She insisted that one must not make sweeping generalizations since, in fact, there were good people even among the Germans.

The teacher, a gentle and mild-mannered person, lost his composure. "What do you know, you foolish child? If you would have seen the way they grabbed my baby out of my arms and killed him, you wouldn't be so magnanimous."

Kiddush Hashem in the non-Jewish world mandates walking a fine line. The counsel of our Sages, "*Kabdeihu v'chashdeihu*—Respect, but be cautious," seems particularly apropos.

Indeed, *sefarim* condemn speaking *lashon hara* of non-Jews, in general. One reason given is that it is an issue of *chillul Hashem*, desecrating the name of Hashem by behaving in ways unbecoming of His people. A second reason is that indulging in negative speech, regardless of the subject, tends to be habit forming. It conditions a person to not only speak disparagingly, but to think negatively. The assumption is that even when prohibitions do not apply, inappropriate behavior cannot be turned off at will. Habits die hard.

Our goal, as Jews, is to maintain the high road in all areas of ethical and spiritual behavior, with everyone with whom we come into contact.

Chapter 45

The Sound of Silence

We live in a world of appearances. Indeed, the Hebrew word for world is *olam*, the root definition of which means "hidden." According to the *sefarim ha'kedoshim*, the reason the Torah describes our world as *olam* is to warn us that what meets the eye is not necessarily the truth. Reality may be hidden beneath the surface and not immediately accessible to the naked eye of the observer.

During a recent visit with my older brother, Rabbi Motel Stein, he shared with us a particularly fascinating teaching from the Baal Shem Tov, the founder of the Chassidic movement. The Baal Shem Tov expounded on what presents as a series of paradoxical statements. He taught the following:

- One can experience a "fast" while eating a bowl of soup.
- One can "dance" while sitting motionlessly.
- One can "speak" while remaining silent.
- One can be in "solitude" even in a crowd.

- One can "self-flagellate," experiencing himself covered with ice, even while under a warm quilt.

The basis for these teachings is the Baal Shem Tov's assertion that the essence of a person is to be found where his thoughts are. Consequently, the common denominator in all of these situations is that what presents outwardly is rarely the whole story. If we understand the Baal Shem Tov correctly, our capacity to judge others is severely limited by our inability to see what lies beneath the surface.

Although each of the Baal Shem Tov's paradoxes demands elaboration, I want to focus specifically on the proposition that one can "speak in silence." So much of our lives is determined by our relationships with our friends and family. How we communicate with them is crucial. And so much of it is, surprisingly, nonverbal.

One of the first things that comes to mind in that regard is the example of my father-in-law, who used to visit the sick in the local hospitals on a daily basis. Every patient, independent of any other, vowed that though my father-in-law said virtually nothing during his brief visit other than a minimal inquiry about their state of health, his mere presence filled them with hope and the desire to live. His kind, compassionate, and saintly visage "silently" spoke volumes.

Other very important expressions of silence abound, each with their unique character and impact. One such example is where our Sages advise us that "the world exists in the merit of the person who keeps his mouth shut during an altercation." Not allowing oneself to be provoked into responding angrily or insultingly during a quarrel is a huge virtue, to the point where one is considered as keeping the universe afloat. A very loud silence, indeed.

Another praiseworthy expression of silence is articulated in *Pirkei Avos* (1:17), where Rabbi Shimon ben Gamliel states that he grew up in the company of Sages, and that he never found a better disposition than silence. In this context, silence serves as a prerequisite for listening, learning, and absorbing wisdom.

Another interesting benefit of silence is promoted by the sobering comment in our holy texts that informs us that every person has a designated number of words allotted to them for their lifetime. It behooves us, therefore, to choose our words judiciously, lest we exhaust our allotment prematurely.

Thankfully, for us mere married mortals who have a hard time keeping our mouths shut, there is also good news. Counterintuitive as it may seem, experts in the field of marital counseling contend that arguing, with both parties verbally venting—if not done to excess, and without name-calling—can actually have a positive effect on the relationship. Ultimately, they insist, arguing can result in the couple coming to a better understanding and getting back on track lovingly. Their conclusion, surprisingly, is that arguing in moderation—*not silence*—can be good for a marriage.

The virtue of silence notwithstanding, there are negative and abusive sides to silence.

Consider the example of Abe and Aviva who came in for counseling. Abe began the conversation by describing Aviva's volatile and explosive mode of expressing frustration. He said that she screamed and yelled in response to any situation that didn't please her. As for himself, Abe related proudly that he always maintained his cool demeanor.

At this point, Aviva could no longer contain herself and took over the conversation. On the verge of tears, Aviva related that Abe's lack of response was insufferably toxic. In effect, Abe "stonewalled" her, giving her the silent treatment, which was far more hurtful, she asserted, than if he would have raised his voice in argument. Abe's stony silence that would last for long periods of time made her feel marginalized, ignored, rejected, manipulated, and worthless.

"But I didn't do anything," Abe protested self-righteously, proving, if anything, Aviva's point that Abe's "doing nothing" was responsible for creating an impenetrable barrier between them. Clearly, Abe's silence spoke louder and more vociferously than harmful words.

It stands to reason that a time-out, such as counting to ten or walking around the block to collect one's thoughts, is advisable before responding to any provocation. Time-outs should not be confused with the detrimental "silent treatment" or "stonewalling" response.

Unquestionably, ongoing stormy encounters of uncontrolled and hurtful verbal outbursts are injurious. Violent eruptions are by no means a better alternative than silence. In truth, neither extreme is acceptable.

The Ribbono Shel Olam has gifted mankind with a unique ability to communicate verbally. Endowed with our holy *neshamah*, Hashem has entrusted us with the capacity to choose when and how to speak, and when and how to be silent. As the Baal Shem Tov taught, we can communicate not only through words, but through silence as well.

May Hashem grant us the strength, wisdom, and discipline to exercise our gift of communication, both audibly and silently, in ways that will bring peace and unity between husbands and wives, parents and children, friends and neighbors, and Klal Yisrael and the nations of the world. May we learn to speak compassionately, from the heart. As our Sages observe, "*Devarim ha'yotzim min ha'lev nichnasim el ha'lev*—Words that come from the heart, enter the heart." That's true of both sound *and* silence.

Conclusion

I n conclusion, I would like to underscore that the Hebrew word for "friend" is "*chaver*," which draws on the Hebrew root "*l'chaber*," to connect.

Chibur, connection, is essential to friendship. The future of friendship in our culture depends on our ability and willingness to, if not eschew, at the very least, minimize, technological modalities that threaten to be a replacement for real, personal, face-to-face interactions. At the end of the day, deep personal interactions are the only vehicles for true *chibur*, for true connection—the indispensable cornerstone of friendship.

Our liturgy exclaims, "*Chaverim kol Yisrael*"—all B'nei Yisrael are fundamentally and inextricably linked as one person, with one heart. That recognition alone has the ability to determine "the future of friendship."

About the Author

Rebbetzin Feige Twerski is the mother of eleven children and many grandchildren, whose number she refuses to divulge. Alongside her husband, Rabbi Michel Twerski, *shlita*, she serves as rebbetzin to her community in Milwaukee and counsels people all over the globe. The rebbetzin is a popular lecturer, speaking on a wide variety of topics to audiences in America and overseas. She is the author of *Ask Rebbetzin Feige* and *Rebbetzin Feige Responds* (Artscroll), as well as *The New Normal* and *The Future of Happiness* (Mosaica Press).

MOSAICA PRESS
BOOK PUBLISHERS

Elegant, Meaningful & Bold

info@MosaicaPress.com
www.MosaicaPress.com

The Mosaica Press team of
acclaimed editors and designers
is attracting some of the most
compelling thinkers and teachers
in the Jewish community today.
Our books are available around
the world.

HARAV YAACOV HABER
RABBI DORON KORNBLUTH